MediaWiki Administrators' Tutorial Guide

Install, manage, and customize your MediaWiki installation

Mizanur Rahman

BIRMINGHAM - MUMBAI

MediaWiki Administrators' Tutorial Guide
Install, manage, and customize your MediaWiki installation

First published: March 2007

Production Reference: 1130307

Published by Packt Publishing Ltd.
32 Lincoln Road
Olton
Birmingham, B27 6PA, UK.

ISBN 978-1-904811-59-6

www.packtpub.com

Cover Image by **Mizanur Rahman** (mizanur.rahman@gmail.com)

Credits

About the Author

Mizanur Rahman graduated in Computer Science from North South University, Bangladesh. His main interests cover a wide area centered on algorithms, distributed and mobile computing, and new web technologies. He has been programming since 1999. He has been a Research Assistant at the Department of Computer Science, North South University, designing and developing web-based solutions for different software for the university. His area of interest includes Java, PHP, AJAX, and other related technologies. He is a moderator of phpXperts — the largest PHP user group in Bangladesh. He is a certified Internet programmer from the largest online testing site, www.Brainbench.com, including a master certificate in PHP. He is currently working as a Senior Software Engineer at Relisource Technologies Ltd, a USA-based software company located in Dhaka, Bangladesh. He is also the technical reviewer of two previous Packt publication books, *vBulletin* and *Smarty*. You can reach him at mizanur.rahman@gmail.com.

I would like to thank my wife Lily and my son Adiyan for their continuous support to complete the book. I want to dedicate my work to my son. I would like to thank my parents and my relatives for their support.

I would like to thank Hasin Hyder and David Barnes for giving me the opportunity to work with Packt Publishing. I would also like to thank all my friends and colleagues for being with me all the time. And finally, I would like to thank Tohin Kashem and Jehad Sarkar, two of my senior colleagues, for their invaluable support throughout my professional career.

And last but not the least, all the people who have worked with me on this book. I am thankful to my reviewers, Nikhil, Peter, and Marc for their valuable inputs. A very special thanks to Nikhil for his great work on the book. A special thanks to Rajlaxmi and Akshara, my technical editors, and others who worked with me in different phases of the book. Without the support of these people, I couldn't have completed the book.

About the Reviewers

Mark Alexander Bain hasn't always been the leading authority on open-source software that you know him as now. Back in the late seventies, he started work as a woodsman at Bowood Estates in Wiltshire. After that he spent a number of years working at Lowther Wildlife Park in Cumbria — it's not clear if his character made him suitable for looking after packs of wolves, or whether the experience made him the way he is now.

In the mid eighties there was a general down turn in the popularity of animal parks in the UK, and Mark found himself out of work with two young sons (Simon and Micheal) — but with a growing interest in programming. His wife had recently bought him the state-of-the-art Sinclair ZX 81, and it was she who suggested that he went to college to study computing.

Mark left college in 1989 and joined Vodafone — then a very small company — where he started writing programs using VAX/VMS. It was shortly after that, that he became addicted to something that was to drastically affect the rest of his life — Unix. His demise was further compounded when he was introduced to Oracle. After that there was no saving him. Over the next few years, Vodafone became the multinational company that it is now, and Mark progressed from Technician to Engineer, and from Engineer to Senior Engineer and finally to Principal Engineer.

At the turn of the century, general ill health made Mark reconsider his career; and his wife again came to his rescue when she saw a job advert for a lecturer at the University of Central Lancashire. It was also she who suggested that he should think about writing.

Today Mark writes regularly for *Linux Format*, *Newsforge.com*, and *Linux Journal*. He's still teaching. And (apparently) he writes books as well.

Peter De Decker is the developer of a MediaWiki extension called "IpbWiki", which is an integration plugin that integrates Invision Power Board with MediaWiki. During the ongoing creation of this extension he has become an expert in understanding the MediaWiki source code and layout.

I would like to thank Mizanur for writing this book and hope that it will further spread the love for this wonderful product.

Table of Contents

Preface

MediaWiki is a free tool to create and manage wiki sites. A wiki simplifies the creation of a collaborative environment where anyone can participate and contribute without having knowledge about web programming. MediaWiki is the most popular open-source software used for creating wiki sites.

Wikipedia, the biggest online content encyclopedia, is powered by MediaWiki. MediaWiki is enriched with an extraordinary ranges of features. With MediaWiki, content creation is simplified and anyone can participate in a wiki without any deep knowledge about the system. MediaWiki is ideal for running a community-driven site where visitors can create accounts, add contents, and interact with each other.

This book is packed with practical steps for you to learn how to build your own MediaWiki-powered website. It will take you through the basics of installing and configuring MediaWiki, advanced formatting, managing contents, administrating your wiki, and customizing the site.

What This Book Covers

In Chapter 1, you will have an overview of a wiki; what it is and when to use it. An overview of Web 2.0 with respect to wikis is also discussed and we then cover MediaWiki's features and a comparision with other available wiki solutions. Based on this, you can make an informed choice on how MediaWiki fits in with your needs.

Chapter 2 walks you through step-by-step instructions to install MediaWiki on a range of platforms. At the end of the chapter you will have your MediaWiki site fully set up, and ready for its wiki journey.

Chapter 3 begins with a detailed view of MediaWiki navigation features. After that, you will learn how to create wiki pages using different approaches and also learn about basic wiki-formatting techniques and editing tools. You will also learn how to create different types of links in MediaWiki.

In Chapter 4, you will learn advanced formatting features to brighten up your content pages. You will start with lists and tables and then go on to learn how to upload files in your wiki site. This chapter gives you a complete overview on using the image functionality of MediaWiki. Towards the end of the chapter, you will learn how to easily represent complex mathematical formulae using Tex.

Chapter 5 will introduce you to the content organization in MediaWiki—it will explain why you need to organize your content and how to do it in MediaWiki. You will also learn about special pages and their uses.

In Chapter 6, you will see how to use wikis in a multi-user environment. Here you will learn how to customize user accounts as per different preferences. This chapter will teach you key techniques such as how to resolve edit conflicts, how to revert changes made by others, and how to communicate with others in a forum.

In Chapter 7, you will be exposed to the administrative side of the MediaWiki. You will learn about different types of access in MediaWiki, and how to grant or deny access to a group of users. By the end of the chapter you will know how to block users, protect pages, and create interwiki links.

In Chapter 8, you will learn to customize MediaWiki. You will learn how to change the layout and appearance of the site. You will be provided with a detailed overview of skin files and walkthroughs on how to change logo and footer, and move around sections in your installed wiki. You will see how you can change the appearance of your site by simply modifying CSS properties. After that, you will learn how to change core files to change the appearance and layout of the site. The last part of the chapter covers the creation of new skins for MediaWiki.

In Chapter 9, you will be introduced to hacking your MediaWiki installation. You will learn about hooks and how to use them without knowing the detailed functionalities of the files. You will see examples of how to write your own hook to extend MediaWiki and also how to write new special pages and customize namespaces.

Chapter 10 discusses the topic of maintening MediaWiki. At the start of the chapter, you will learn how to deploy MediaWiki, and back up the database and files. You will also learn about importing files and databases from another wiki site while maintaining your site.

Chapter 11 is dedicated to a few cool hacks—namely ones for a calendar, YouTube integration, multiple uploads, category clouds, and Google maps. The chapter provides download links and short descriptions and you are shown how to integrate these hacks into your site.

What You Need for This Book

To use this book, you will need the latest version of Mediawiki, which can be freely downloaded from `http://www.mediawiki.org`. The steps to get Mediawiki up and running are detailed in Chapter 2.

In order to install MediaWiki, we need four components—a web server, a MySQL database server, PHP 5, and MediaWiki files. In this book we assume that you have experience of installing web server, database server, and PHP, or already have them in your machine. But it takes you on a detailed ride through the installation of MediaWiki files.

Conventions

In this book, you will find a number of styles of text that distinguish between different kinds of information. Here are some examples of these styles, and an explanation of their meanings.

There are three styles for code. Code words in text are shown as follows: "Include the following line at the end of your `LocalSettings.php` file."

A block of code will be set as follows:

```
<gallery>
Image:ghostmap.jpg
Image:Ghost map small.jpg|[[Nevada_map | Nevada Ghost Map]]
Image:UK ghost map.gif | UK ghost Sighted
```

When we wish to draw your attention to a particular part of a code block, the relevant lines or items will be made bold:

```
|+ Story Listing
!# !! Story Title !! Author !! Submission Date
|- style="background:white; color:black"
! 1.
| style="width:300px" |The Ghost of the Old Mathematician
| J. David
| 12/09/2006
```

Any command-line input and output is written as follows:

```
>CREATE DATABASE `mediawiki`;
```

New terms and **important words** are introduced in a bold-type font. Words that you see on the screen, in menus or dialog boxes for example, appear in our text like this: "There is a link that says **set up the wiki**."

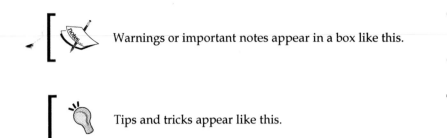

Warnings or important notes appear in a box like this.

Tips and tricks appear like this.

Reader Feedback

Feedback from our readers is always welcome. Let us know what you think about this book, what you liked or may have disliked. Reader feedback is important for us to develop titles that you really get the most out of.

To send us general feedback, simply drop an email to feedback@packtpub.com, making sure to mention the book title in the subject of your message.

If there is a book that you need and would like to see us publish, please send us a note in the **SUGGEST A TITLE** form on www.packtpub.com or email suggest@packtpub.com.

If there is a topic that you have expertise in and you are interested in either writing or contributing to a book, see our author guide on www.packtpub.com/authors.

Customer Support

Now that you are the proud owner of a Packt book, we have a number of things to help you to get the most from your purchase.

Downloading the Example Code for the Book

Visit http://www.packtpub.com/support, and select this book from the list of titles to download any example code or extra resources for this book. The files available for download will then be displayed.

The downloadable files contain instructions on how to use them.

Errata

Although we have taken every care to ensure the accuracy of our c ts, mistakes
do happen. If you find a mistake in one of our books—maybe a mis n text or
code—we would be grateful if you would report this to us. By doing you can
save other readers from frustration, and help to improve subsequent ons of
this book. If you find any errata, report them by visiting `http://www.` tpub.
`com/support`, selecting your book, clicking on the **Submit Errata** link, a ntering
the details of your errata. Once your errata are verified, your submission l be
accepted and the errata are added to the list of existing errata. The existing rata can
be viewed by selecting your title from `http://www.packtpub.com/suppor`

Questions

You can contact us at `questions@packtpub.com` if you are having a problem with
some aspect of the book, and we will do our best to address it.

1

About MediaWiki

Before we get down to starting on wiki engines (and wikis in general), I would like to take a minute to present a case in point—the wiki that started it all.

Wikipedia

The free encyclopedia that anyone can edit is the slogan of Wikipedia, an online encyclopedia. Wikipedia is a great online resource center for everyone and every purpose. It is the biggest multilingual encyclopedia available online, containing over 2 million articles and still growing. You won't be surprised to hear that many of us have first heard the term wiki from the site Wikipedia. Have you ever wondered what software is managing such a huge number of articles and performing flawlessly? The software is none other than MediaWiki, a wiki engine that manages wiki site. Now let's see what a wiki means.

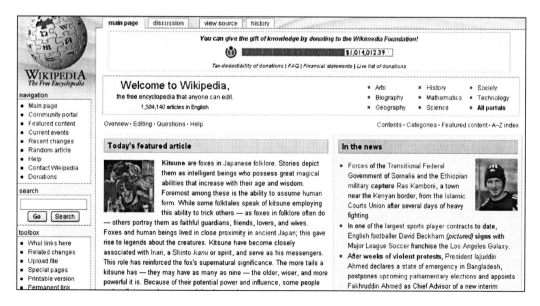

Wiki

A wiki is a browser-based collaborative writing environment, in which a community may amass and exchange information on particular topics, and to which anyone may contribute without having web programming skills. In other words, a wiki is a piece of software that is used for collaborative content creation.

Different people have different ideas about what a wiki really is, but whichever definition we take, a wiki is software that handles complex problems in a simple manner.

According to Leuf and Cunningham, the creators of the original wiki concept, "a wiki is a freely expandable collection of interlinked web pages, a hypertext system for storing and modifying information—a database, where each page can easily be edited by any user with a forms-capable web browser client". The content can be directly linked to that found in other wikis and in web documents.

In many situations, we need something collaborative on the Internet. We should be able to contribute to a particular discussion and ensure that everyone has the ability to participate. Wiki gives us this opportunity and flexibility to perform such tasks. To use a wiki, we do not have to be a webmaster or have knowledge about web programming. We do not need any special software for that. Just open a web browser, go to a wiki site and start writing. We neither have to wait for a webmaster to upload our contents and share with others, nor do we have to wait for any administrator to approve our contents to be shown. We can do it ourselves instantly.

When to Use a Wiki

As we have just discussed, a wiki is used to create collaborative or community sites, and it will not be wise to use a wiki site for personal purposes. We can use wiki when we need to build something for the community, where more than one person will share their views, knowledge, and opinions. We can use wiki for brainstorming, a community forum based on specific topics, developing frequently ask questions (FAQs), a knowledge base, course management and project management, family histories, planning, etc.

These are the possibilities that we can implement using a wiki, but is this the only reason we will be using a wiki? The answer is no, not at all. Suppose we are developing an open-source project where people from different locations are contributing. Now to build a collaborative system, we might need some people working on the collaboration process, to take information from each contributor, make a page, and publish it for the other contributors, or need the contributor to mail the findings and changes to the other contributors.

There are two bottlenecks in these situations. For the first one, there is no necessity of collecting information from contributors and presenting information to others. It is just a waste of time. For the second one, think about the others who join in later for the development; how will they know all the information about the previous contributions? The answer is someone will demonstrate all the things to the newcomer and keep doing it again and again as new contributors join the program in the future. But does it really make any sense? A wiki-based site can take care of all these painful tasks itself. We do not need anyone to take notes from contributors and publish them online. Each contributor can do it himself or herself by adding, editing contents in the wiki site. It is the easiest job on earth to work with a wiki site.

Wiki versus Blog, Forum, and CMS

A question could arise in your minds at this stage: Can't we do the same task using a CMS (content management system), forum, blog, or other community software? The answer is yes. But wait! Don't jump to any conclusion yet. If we think a forum, blog, and CMS are easy solutions for this, then a wiki will be an even easier solution for the problem. Let's explore a few simple differences:

Feature	Blog	Forum	CMS	Wiki
Posting/ Editing content	Usually done by the blog owner. Visitors can post comments on a particular post, but it requires approval from the blog owner before showing to the site.	Any registered member can post a message but in general you might need approval of the administrator for that. Visitors or other users can reply on the message, but cannot change the original post.	Only an administrator can post the content. Other users can view the content.	Anyone can add or edit content easily without any intervention from the administrator.
Contributing	The blog owner writes the content and other comments on it. So the blog owner is the main contributor.	For a particular topic, the participants are the contributors to the topic, but only the admin can change the core topic content.	In CMS, the administrator or the privileged to create contents are the contributors. Others can not comment or edit the contents.	In a wiki everyone is a contributor. He or she can edit anyone's content, and even complete the uncompleted contents.

In general a wiki can be classified as a very simple tool for managing your content. The wiki stands out among forums, blogs, and CMS for its simplicity. A wiki gives you the flexibility to do more things that any other single piece of software can provide. You can use wiki pages to serve your content like a CMS. You can use wiki talk pages to create discussions like in a forum. A wiki might not have the all the features that you can have in a CMS and forum software, but it gives you many options so that you can play around and create feature-rich sites with basic tools. It is just like a blank canvas, and you can portray anything you want.

Is a Wiki Right for You?

The answer is: it solely depends on your requirements. If you are planning to build an e-commerce site, then a wiki is not a good solution for you. If you are looking to build a personal information site, then a wiki is not the right option for you. There can be many other situations for which a wiki would not be a suitable solution. However, whenever you want to build a collaborative site, where every voice can be heard, you can consider a wiki as a good solution.

If you need to manage large content you can easily choose a wiki since the largest online encyclopaedia, Wikipedia, uses a wiki to manage such large content. Content management has been transformed to a simple task after arrival of wikis in the scenario.

Nowadays open-source projects are blooming. We have thousands of open-source projects where millions of people are participating, contributing, and using projects. The open-source community is growing rapidly and in order to manage such a large community, many open-source projects have their own sites for supporting users and contributors with range of knowledgebases, development materials, news, announcements, etc. It is a very hard job to manage such large numbers of users and amounts of content. That is why many of the most popular open-source projects have shifted to wiki solutions for their content management issues. Mozilla wiki (http://www.wiki.mozilla.org), Linux Fedora Core wiki (http://www.fedoraproject.org/wiki/), the Eclipse Project wiki (http://wiki.eclipse.org/), and the AJAX Patterns site (http://www.ajaxpatterns.org) are a few names to mention for their effective wiki use.

So if you are looking to build a knowledge-based site you can definitely choose a wiki as the perfect solution.

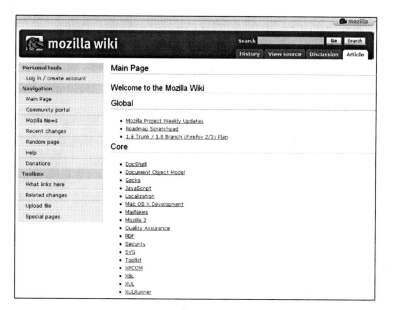

You can use a wiki for creating information-based site like. Wikitravel (`http://www.wikitravel.com`) is popular site run by a wiki in order to serve traveling information to travelers from around the world. You can use wiki for creating news sites as well as a dictionary. The bottom line of the discussion is that if your content is large, then it is always better to use a wiki.

Web 2.0

With the bursting of the dot-com bubble in 2001, many things happened to the web world. Lots of new sites came out and made their presence felt in the world of web. New concepts and new vision gave the Web a new life. That's what we call the Web 2.0. It is a move from the complex services aimed at attracting customers, to simple friendly tools aimed at helping people benefit from each other's presence and skills.

Today, the Web is not just few HTML pages for information sharing. Today's Web is much more mature and focused on a particular area. Perhaps the best known word about Web 2.0 is AJAX (Asynchronous JavaScript and XML). Google was the first to introduce this concept to the web world and it was grasped within no time by everyone. In the early web scenarios, we focused more on technologies like double-click, personal websites, content management system, screen scrapping, etc. However, our views have changed after the arrival of Web 2.0. We are now focusing more on making the Web a platform to develop web-based applications.

The core competencies of Web 2.0 are:

- It is a service not a packaged product.
- It is an architecture where any one can participate.
- It has cost-effective scalability.
- It has mixable data sources and data transformation.
- It is focused to create software above the level of a single device.
- It harnesses collective intelligence.

Web 2.0 and Wiki

As we have seen from the previous discussion, Web 2.0 is the next big thing for the web world. If we think of Web 2.0 as a medium for collaboration, then here are the key concepts that build the thought:

- Users control the processing of information and generation of new forms of expression, as well as subscriptions and relationships.
- Makes the Web a point of presence by creating internet-mediated social environments with collective activities and participation.
- Is more focused on user engagement and rich user experiences.
- It is about participation and democracy for the users that encourages users to add value to the application they are using. It is a media revolution where you can hear the voice of the crowd rather than a single voice.

Now we put the beads together for a wiki to fit it into the Web 2.0 paradigm:

- A wiki is a piece of application that is used for collaborative participation.
- Users are the primary contributors for a wiki-based site.
- Users process information and publish it for all.
- It is all about people's voices that we hear.
- People are breaking the barrier of the geographical border and creating a new citizenship in the web world.

About MediaWiki

MediaWiki is the wiki implementation used by Wikipedia and the other Wikimedia resources. These are, probably, the largest and most successful wikis. It is robust and has proved itself with the public. The markup style is already known to a large number of wiki users. The display is easy to navigate, and it is simple to format text from the toolbar. MediaWiki offers a lot of features, including an optional file upload feature, a very comprehensive markup, very good internationalization support (even supporting bi-directional text), version control, a search feature, back-links, mathematical equation support, and page names that can consist of any characters.

MediaWiki is written in PHP and uses a MySQL database. MediaWiki installation is incredibly simple, especially considering its complexity. It involves setting up a MySQL database, unpacking the distribution, making a certain directory there writable, and accessing a configuration script. It has a lot of configuration options, and you can configure it to your heart's desire. It is built to work in almost any web-hosting environment that gives you MySQL and PHP.

The MediaWiki syntax is both very rich and flexible. You can even use some HTML tags instead of the regular markup, which is useful if you cannot recall the original markup immediately. It has many features that may make it overkill for some sites, but that largely depends on your requirements and it is not necessary for you to use all the available features.

MediaWiki Features

Let us have a look at a few features of MediaWiki:

- **Easy navigation system**: MediaWiki provides an easy navigation system with options such as searching, **Go** button, **random page**, **Special pages**, and **Printable version** of a page. The entire navigation system is present on the page, so you can quickly browse through it.

- **Editing, formatting, and referencing**: MediaWiki provides an easy way to edit, format, and reference pages with other pages. It also gives us the option to track changes. Since it is a multi-user environment, tracking changes is a key feature to manage the content properly.

- **Look and feel change**: Users can change the look and feel of a wiki site using MediaWiki. Users can change skins and styles for their individual pages.

- **File uploading**: MediaWiki gives you an option to add file upload capabilities to your pages. This is a nice option to make it a complete content management system. It also gives you flexibility to decide the allowable file extensions that can be uploaded by users and also a block list of file extensions.

- **Multilanguage support**: MediaWiki supports many languages and UTF-8. So you can implement MediaWiki in different languages. Many sites such as Wikipedia use a multilingual version, which allows you to read and write different languages using the same piece of software.

- **User management**: MediaWiki has a built-in user management system where you can create new logins and assign user privileges. You can also customize privileges for user types in order to fit your security needs.

- **Syndication**: MediaWiki supports web syndication by providing RSS syndication for many special pages such as `Special:Newpages` and `Special:Recentchanges`. Syndication benefits both the websites providing information and the websites displaying it. It gives the option to grow your site rapidly in the web world.

Available Wiki Software

There are lots of open-source and commercial wiki software packages available online. You can search with Google with the wiki keyword and can find lots of wiki software. Here are a few popular wiki software packages available:

- **DokuWiki**: DokuWiki is a simple wiki engine based on PHP and can be used to create any type of document. It is simple and standards compliant. It is suitable for small companies, development teams, and user groups. The most interesting part of this wiki is that it does not have any database.

  As a result all the data is saved in a plain text file. The syntax is very simple yet powerful enough to create any type of content. Key features include: simplified editing, linking, support for image and other files, plug-ins support to extend wiki functionality.

- **PhpWiki**: PhpWiki is a clone of original WikiWikiWeb. It was the first wiki software written in PHP and was released in 1999. It supports a majority of the databases. The installation process is very simple and gives you what you look for in an out-of-the-box solution. It supports plug-ins in order to increase functionality. It is suitable for freeform discussion-based site creation and also for collaborative development sites.

- **PmWiki**: PmWiki is a PHP-based wiki that does not require any database. It is very easy to install and to extend its functionality. It supports a template system in order to change the look and feel of the website as well as the functionality to a great extent. It also provides an access control system in order to protect site pages or groups of pages by enabling a password-protected mechanism. It also gives ample opportunity to customize the site as well as extend its functionality using plug-ins.

- **QwikiWiki**: QwikiWiki is another wiki system written in PHP and does not require any SQL database in order to operate. It uses cookies and its own file system in order to process and manage files. It has some key features like file uploading, a template system, and an access control system.

- **Wikipage**: It is small, but a wiki standard, easy-to-use system. Wikipage is more secure than Tipwiki. It has password-protection support for access control, multilanguage and multisite support. Other common features include file uploading, table support etc.

- **TWiki**: TWiki is a flexible, powerful, and easy-to-use enterprise collaboration platform and knowledge management system. It is a structured wiki written in Perl. It is typically used to run a project development space, a document management system, a knowledge base, or any other groupware tool, on an intranet or on the Internet. It does not require any database since the data are stored in file system. It has a powerful plug-ins system with more than 200 plug-ins available to use such as spreadsheet, image gallery, slide shows, drawings, charts, graphs, etc.

- **Kwiki**: Kwiki is perhaps the simplest to install, most modular, and easiest to extend. It is written in Perl and also available in CPAN. Other than providing basic wiki features, Kwiki by default offers slide shows, page backups, privacy options, and blog capabilities that are not found in any other wiki. It supports a plug-ins system in order to extend functionality.

- **MoinMoin**: MoinMoin is written in Python and has been derived from the PikiPiki wiki engine. This wiki uses a flat file and folder in order to save data. It does not require any database for operation. It is extensible and customizable. It supports sub-pages, Unicode, RSS feed, a template system, theme support, an access control list, and an anti-spam feature.

How MediaWiki Fits your Need

If you are looking for a wiki as a solution, then MediaWiki is a better choice. It has a cool feature set and offers flexibility. Let's tailor MediaWiki features in order to fit your needs:

- **Editing is simplified**: Every page contains an **Edit** link on the top navigation bar, which will take you to a very simple editing screen upon clicking. When you finish making changes, submit them by clicking the **SUBMIT** button, and, voila! Your changes show up on the site. Can editing be simpler than that? I don't think so.

- **Use of simple markup**: When you edit an HTML content item, it is always difficult if you do not have proper knowledge of HTML tags. Nowadays WYSIWYG editors take away the pain but still in some cases you need to work with HTML markup. What if the program does this for you? You don't have to remember complex tags. Yes, that is why MediaWiki is so simplified. It has its own type of syntax, which makes the editing a simpler job and the proper HTML tag conversion is done by the system. MediaWiki will solve this problem by writing the HTML for you. All you need is to learn a few simple markup rules. These rules are designed to make wiki markup easy for general users to write and adopt.

- **Recording histories**: MediaWiki will save a copy of your old pages and lets you revert to an older version of a page if you need to. In fact, MediaWiki will display a comparison, called a diff, which shows you the exact changes you have made or someone else has to your page over time.

- **Simplifying creating links**: MediaWiki stores your entire website's content in an internal hypertext database. MediaWiki knows about every page you have and about every link you make. When you are using MediaWiki, you don't have to worry about the location of files or the format of your tags. Simply name the page, and MediaWiki will automatically create a link for you. You can create links within your wiki or to some other wiki as well as to the web world. Creating links cannot be simpler than the way MediaWiki does it.

- **Simplifying creating new pages**: MediaWiki links you to pages that don't yet exist. Click on a link that points to a nonexistent page, and the wiki will ask you for the initial content to be placed in the page. If you submit some initial content, then the wiki will create the page. All links to that page (not just the one you clicked) will now point to the newly-created page. That is the simplest way of creating a new page in MediaWiki. You don't even have to bother to create the page, save it, and then link it from another page. You can do it in a single shoot.

- **Simplifying site organization**: MediaWiki uses a database in order to manage the hypertext of the site. As a result you can organize your page however you want. Many content management systems require you to plan classifications for your content before you actually create it. This can be helpful, but only if you are looking for a rigid structure. With MediaWiki you can organize your page into categories and namespaces if you want, and you can also try other things. Instead of designing the site structure, many wiki sites just let the structure grow with the content and the links inside their content. But you don't have to have it either way. Visitors can navigate the site by following a storyline, drilling down through a hierarchy, or they can just browse with the natural flow of the internal links. MediaWiki helps you to get out of this nightmare and without any such a complex site structure.

- **Tracking all your stuff**: Using MediaWiki, you can track everything in your site, because MediaWiki stores everything in a database and it knows about all your links and all your pages. So it's easy for MediaWiki to show back-links, a list of all the pages that link to the current page. It also stores your document history in order to list recent changes. It can even show a list of recent changes to pages that link to the current page.

- **Opportunity for collaborative communities**: The core concept of MediaWiki is to create a collaborative community. MediaWiki allows anyone to click the **Edit** button and change the website. While this may seem odd, many wikis are able to do this successfully without major issues in terms of vandalism. Remember, MediaWiki stores the history of each page. So in case of an act of vandalism, the original content can quickly be reset. MediaWiki gives you the option to handle this challenge differently. You can make the site completely open, and to curb vandalism, you can make restricted access to the site so that only register users can do the editing or you can even set a different reporting system to stop such activities. How you deal with this challenge depends on what you plan to use the wiki for.

Summary

In this chapter we have learned about the basics of wikis and their usefulness, the features of MediaWiki and a bit about Web 2.0. We have learned that a wiki is an application that is used for collaborative content development with a very easy-to-use user interface. In the next chapter we will see how to install MediaWiki on our system.

2
Installing MediaWiki

In this chapter you will learn how to install MediaWiki on your local machine, which could be running either Windows or Linux, and also on a hosted web server. The installation process is very simple and easy to perform so let's quickly jump to it.

Prerequisites

In order to install MediaWiki, we need the following components:

- Web server (Apache or IIS)
- Database server (MySQL version 4.0 and above or PostgreSQL 8.1 and above)
- PHP 5.0 and above
- The latest MediaWiki files

Since this book is about MediaWiki, we are not going to learn about the installation of a web server, database server, or even PHP. We will assume that you have installed the latest version of Apache web server, MySQL database server, and the latest version of PHP on your machine. Please note that support for PostgreSQL is very new and not as well tested as that for MySQL, so we will only discuss MySQL here. We would also need to download the MediaWiki files which we will see in the next section.

Downloading MediaWiki

The latest version of MediaWiki can be downloaded at MediaWiki's downloads page: http://www.mediawiki.org/wiki/Download.

 When you download the MediaWiki ZIP file it will show an extension similar to .tar.gz. Make sure you retain this extension because some browsers tend to just keep a .tar extension at the end of the file, which can create problems while unzipping.

Upload the MediaWiki Files to your Server

When the download is complete, uncompress the .tar file. You can use the following command to uncompress the file on a Linux-based system:

```
tar -xvzf mediawiki-*.tar.gz
```

For a Windows-based system, you can use do the same using an extracting tool like WinZip or 7-Zip.

Once the extraction is complete you will have a folder named MediaWiki-*.

 The * symbol refers to the version used. In our case it will be MediaWiki-1.9.0

Now we have to move this folder to a web-accessible location, which will be referred as the "root" of our installation. For Apache, we will move it into the htdocs directory.

You can place it in the root, and if you have access to the httpd.conf file, you can make a symlink for the folder.

If you are using a hosting company to host the site, it is usually better to create a directory under the /www/ folder in the filesystem such as /wiki and upload all the files from the extracted folder in your local drive into this folder.

 MediaWiki filenames are case sensitive. So files should be named as they are in the extracted folder.

The extracted file will generate a lot of files, spread over dozens of directories. Be careful when uploading them to a remote server. If the transfer is interrupted, you might have missing or incomplete files. You may have to retry your upload several times, especially if you have an unreliable connection. It is very important to upload all the files to the server for proper operation.

Creating a MySQL Database

Since MediaWiki uses a MySQL database server, before installing MediaWiki in your system make sure you create a database for it. This will be easier if you have root access to your server. Let us call this database mediawiki. You can run the following command in your MySQL command window to create the database:

```
>CREATE DATABASE `mediawiki`;
```

It is also necessary to create a user to access this database. You can do this from your MySQL server on your local machine or in your hosted server. Let us create a user name **wikiadmin** to access this database.

Changing Permissions of the Config Folder

It is very important to know that, before starting the installation process, the config folder under the extracted folder must be writable. To make it so, go to the folder that contains the MediaWiki files for installation. You will see lots of folders there, with one named config. Make this directory writable, as the web server will write some setup files inside this folder during installation.

A simpler but much less secure approach is to run the chmod o+w config command. This means you need to set the permissions of the config directory to "world writable". This is the same as chmod 777.

Another way to change the permissions is to use your FTP client—read the help to figure out how to set the permissions (e.g. with the "Core FTP" client you simply right-click on the config directory and select properties. A dialogue box will appear and easily allows you to change the permissions to 777).

Another way to set permissions is to use your web host's "control panel" to access the file manager functions. If you are not allowed to set the permissions to 777, try setting them to 755 or 775 instead.

If you are not familiar with file permissions in a Linux system then chmod and 777 or 755 will not make any sense to you. To give you a brief idea, chmod is used to change file permissions. In general there are three types of user groups for a particular file or directory: owner, group, and others. Each of the user groups can have three permissions: read, write, and execute. These permissions are either on or off. So for each group we can write something like this as file permission in binary format: 111.

111 means for the particular group of users read permission is allowed (which is the first bit), write permission is allowed (the second bit), and also execution permission is allowed (the last bit). And 111 in binary format is equal to decimal 7. So a decimal value 5 (binary 101) will indicate that only read and execution permission is allowed. Now I believe 777 or 755 make sense to you. The first digit is for the owner, the second one is for the group, and the third one is for others. So a 755 permission means the owner will have all the privileges whereas the group and others will have only read and execution privileges and no write privileges.

The Installation Process

Open a web browser and visit the location where the wiki files reside. For the local machine just type the following URL in your web browser address bar (assuming that you are installing your wiki in a folder called mediawiki):

```
http://localhost/mediawiki/
```

If you are installing it on a hosting server, enter the domain name followed by your wiki installation folder to install the application. For example: if your site name is www.mysite.com, then you will open the URL www.mysite.com/mediawiki/ in your web browser.

Once you go to the URL specified, the page will lead you to the installation process. The installation process is very simple and easy to perform. Just perform the following steps:

1. When you go to the specified URL, you will see a welcome window similar to the following:

    There is a link that says **set up the wiki**. Click this link to move to the next stage, which is the actual installation process.

2. When you are in the installation section, the installation script will automatically check for the environment settings and will show the status of the required programs and settings in the server. If all the requirements are met then you can proceed with the installation. A message — **Environment checked. You can install MediaWiki** — will be shown at the bottom of the environment checking section in order to indicate that. If anything is missing, then it will show a red error message and you need to fix it before continuing the installation process.

Here is the screen that will be shown for environment checking:

3. Scroll down to the **Site configuration** options. This is the main installation process file, so be careful while entering the details. You need to fill in the following:

Wiki name: This is used for setting up the site information. For the time being just enter **www.mysite.com** (used as an example) in the **Wiki name box**. This field is mandatory.

Contact e-mail field: If you want you can also put your email address in the **Contact e-mail field**, this email address will be used as a default address for password reminders and error reporting in the site.

Language: Choose the desired language support for your site from the list. The default is **English.**

Copyright/license: Based on your requirement you can choose any of the options provided in this section. For our setup we will use the default one (**no license metadata**).

Site config

Wiki name: [   ]   Must not be blank or "MediaWiki"

Preferably a short word without punctuation, i.e. "Wikipedia".
Will appear as the namespace name for "meta" pages, and throughout the interface.

Contact e-mail: [   ]

Displayed to users in some error messages, used as the return address for password reminders, and used as the default sender
address of e-mail notifications.

Language: [en - English   ▼]

Select the language for your wiki's interface. Some localizations aren't fully complete. Unicode (UTF-8) is used for all localizations.

Copyright/license: ⦿ No license metadata
  ○ GNU Free Documentation License 1.2 (Wikipedia-compatible)
  ○ A Creative Commons license - choose

A notice, icon, and machine-readable copyright metadata will be displayed for the license you pick.

Admin username: [WikiSysop   ]
Password: [   ]   Must not be blank
Password confirm: [   ]

An admin can lock/delete pages, block users from editing, and do other maintenance tasks.
A new account will be added only when creating a new wiki database.

Shared memory caching: ⦿ No caching
  ○ Memcached
Memcached servers: [   ]

Using a shared memory system such as Turck MMCache, APC, eAccelerator, or Memcached will speed up MediaWiki significantly.
Memcached is the best solution but needs to be installed. Specify the server addresses and ports in a comma-separated list. Only
use Turck shared memory if the wiki will be running on a single Apache server.

Admin username and **Password**: This is the **Sysop** account information. A Sysop is a user with very high-level system privileges such as locking and removing pages, blocking suspected IP addresses, and performing various setup tasks. You might be familiar with the terms owner and administrator for a site. Sysop is a synonymous term for administrator and owner. So this account information is very critical and must be filled out during the installation process.

Shared memory caching: If you have any shared memory set up for the server to cache pages, you can enter the information in the shared memory option field. We will learn more about caching in the administration section later in this book.

4. The next block of configuration is about **E-mail, e-mail notification and authentication setup.** This configuration enables general email setup, user to user email system, and email notification system setup. The installation file itself contains good explanation for the options. Before selecting any option, you can read the informational text below the option. For our setup we will keep the default settings as they are. You can configure your server the way you want.

E-mail, e-mail notification and authentication setup

E-mail features (global): ◉ Enabled
　　　　　　　　　　　　　○ Disabled

　　　　Use this to disable all e-mail functions (password reminders, user-to-user e-mail and e-mail notifications) if sending mail doesn't work on your server.

User-to-user e-mail: ◉ Enabled
　　　　　　　　　　　○ Disabled

　　　　The user-to-user e-mail feature (Special:Emailuser) lets the wiki act as a relay to allow users to exchange e-mail without publicly advertising their e-mail address.

E-mail notification about ○ Disabled
changes: ○ Enabled for changes to user discussion pages only
　　　　　　　◉ Enabled for changes to user discussion pages, and to pages on watchlists (not recommended for large wikis)

　　　　For this feature to work, an e-mail address must be present for the user account, and the notification options in the user's preferences must be enabled. Also note the authentication option below. When testing the feature, keep in mind that your own changes will never trigger notifications to be sent to yourself.

　　　　There are additional options for fine tuning in /includes/DefaultSettings.php; copy these to your LocalSettings.php and edit them there to change them.

E-mail address ○ Disabled
authentication: ◉ Enabled

　　　　If this option is enabled, users have to confirm their e-mail address using a magic link sent to them whenever they set or change it, and only authenticated e-mail addresses can receive mails from other users and/or change notification mails. Setting this option is **recommended** for public wikis because of potential abuse of the e-mail features above.

---

5. Now we are in the most critical part of the setup, **Database config.** The database configuration section is the last but most important part of the whole installation process. Recall that a few pages back we set up a database in the MySQL database server for our wiki use.

Database config

Database type:	⊙ MySQL
Database host:	localhost

If your database server isn't on your web server, enter the name or IP address here.

Database name:	mediawiki
DB username:	wikiadmin
DB password:	Must not be blank
DB password confirm:	

If you only have a single user account and database available, enter those here. If you have database root access (see below) you can specify new accounts/databases to be created. This account will not be created if it pre-exists. If this is the case, ensure that it has SELECT, INSERT, UPDATE and DELETE permissions on the MediaWiki database.

Superuser account:	☐ Use superuser account
Superuser name:	root
Superuser password:	

If the database user specified above does not exist, or does not have access to create the database (if needed) or tables within it, please check the box and provide details of a superuser account, such as **root**, which does.

MySQL specific options:

Database table prefix:	

If you need to share one database between multiple wikis, or MediaWiki and another web application, you may choose to add a prefix to all the table names to avoid conflicts.

Avoid exotic characters; something like mw_ is good.

Database charset — Select one:
- ⊙ Backwards-compatible UTF-8
- ○ Experimental MySQL 4.1/5.0 UTF-8
- ○ Experimental MySQL 4.1/5.0 binary

EXPERIMENTAL: You can enable explicit Unicode charset support for MySQL 4.1 and 5.0 servers. This is not well tested and may cause things to break. **If upgrading an older installation, leave in backwards-compatible mode.**

[**Install MediaWiki!**]

We need to provide that information over here:

Database name: The name of the MySQL database you have created earlier. In this case the database we used is **mediawiki**.

DB username: The username used for accessing your wiki MySQL database.

DB password: The user password for accessing your wiki MySQL database.

Database table prefix: Though it is optional, it is a very good option to have a database table prefix. It allows you to install more than one wiki using the same databases. This option also gives you the opportunity to create MediaWiki tables under an existing database with the tables distinguished by our desired prefix. The last option is to provide a root password for the database. You can provide the information if you have it and click the **Install MediaWiki!** button. If you don't have the information then use the password you have used to create the database and user for the MediaWiki database.

If you are using a hosting service, please note that the database name and database username may have a prefix (normally the userID given by your hosting provider). For example, if you have created a database named mediawiki with username wikiadmin and your userID for the site is mysiteid (given by your hosting provider), you should enter the database name and database username as mysiteid_mediawiki and mysiteid_wikiadmin respectively.

6. After providing all the information you are just a click away from installing MediaWiki. Click the **Install MediaWiki!** button to start the installation process, and sit back and wait for the server to finish the installation process. If something is wrong, then the server will come back to the setup page for the information. If all the information provided is correct then the server will take some time to set up the site. Usually the time taken is between 5 and 15 seconds. Once the installation is done, you will see a success message in green—**Installation successful!**—at the bottom of the page.

7. During the installation process a file named LocalSettings.php is created by the server. It is located under the config folder. To ensure that this file is created, we had to change the config folder's properties to make the folder writable. Before clicking the link to view the wiki homepage, move the LocalSettings.php file to the root folder. After doing so, you have to click on **this link** provided in the success page to start the wiki.

If the installation is successful, the following screen will be shown:

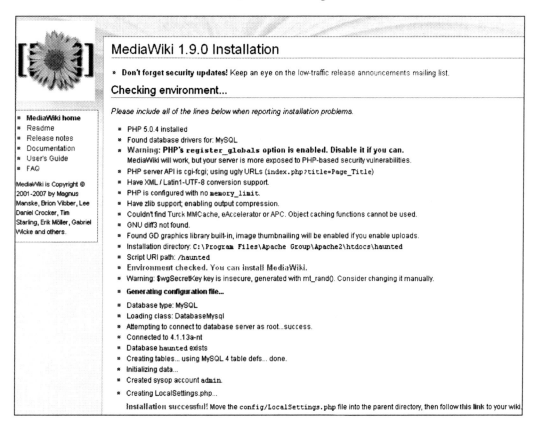

 Remember to move the `LocalSettings.php` file (not to copy the file) to the main wiki site. It is very important to move the `LocalSettings.php` file, because when you try to load MediaWiki site, if the file is still found in the `config` folder, then the system will assume that MediaWiki is not properly installed and it will show you the message that `Localsettings.php` file must be moved to the root directory.

First Look at our Installed Wiki Site

At the end of the installation success message, a link is provided to go to the installed wiki site. Click on **this link** for your first glance at the wiki site. You will see a window similar to this:

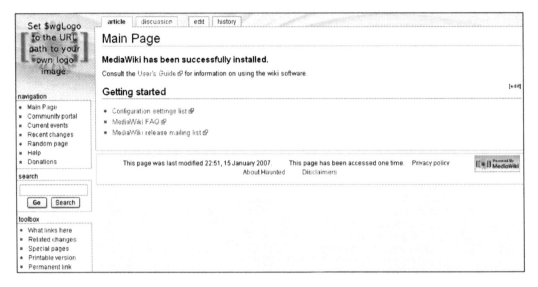

We can divide the first page into few categories. The first is the left navigation menu with the logo option including the toolbox and search box. The second is the main body section and the third is the footer section.

Haunted: Our Sample Site

Since we are learning about MediaWiki, our main focus will be to build a nice wiki with lots of features. In order to achieve that, in the whole book we will focus on only one example wiki site where we will apply our changes in order to make a complete product at the end of the book. The topic set for the wiki is "Haunted—a ghost hunters paradise". We will create a site for the ghost hunters all around the world, where people can share their real-life experiences, stories, and images, discuss different ghost topics, and most importantly, they can share their findings and knowledge with others. We will enjoy creating such a site.

Summary

In this chapter we have learned about the installation and configuration of MediaWiki. In the next chapter we will start our wiki journey by creating new pages and learning the wiki syntax.

3
Starting MediaWiki

In the previous chapters we learned about MediaWiki features and its installation. Now let us get some hands-on experience on how to use MediaWiki. This chapter will give us the basic steps of writing a wiki and its syntax as well as its formatting. So let's start the journey. However, before starting let us see what we are going to learn in this chapter:

- MediaWiki navigation
- Creating and editing pages
- Options for formatting pages
- Linking between different pages

A Closer Look at the MediaWiki Navigation

Before writing a wiki, we need to learn about the MediaWiki navigation system. This will help us to understand things properly and also to operate the site smoothly.

So, when we open the first page of MediaWiki just after the installation, we will see the following page:

We have divided the page into five subsections to make things simpler. So let's explore each section according to the numbering done on the image:

1. Navigation
2. Toolbox
3. Login section
4. Main body section
5. Footer

Navigation

First in our list of sections is the left-side **navigation** area, which consists of navigation links and a search section. The navigation contains links to a few common pages such as **Main Page, Community portal, Current events, Recent changes, Random page, Help**, etc.

Now let us have a look at a very brief summary of the each link:

Main Page

In MediaWiki, the **Main Page** indicates the **homepage** of the site. Usually a homepage is the first page of a site and contains a snapshot of the contents and links of the site. The **Main Page** link of the left navigation bar links to the main page of the site. At any point of time if we want to go back to the home page we can click the **Main Page** link. The Main Page from Wikipedia is as shown below:

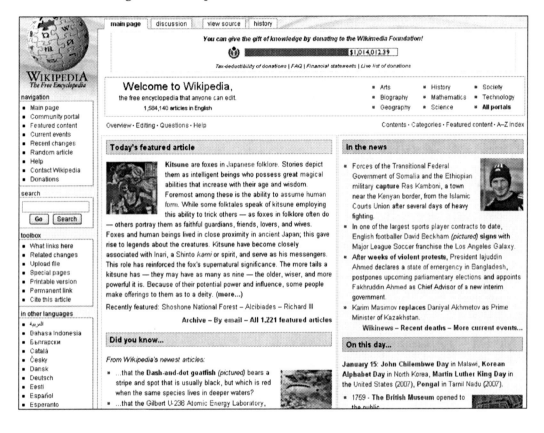

Community Portal

The **Community portal** link takes you to the section where you can view the community site information (if there is any for the current site). Usually the community portal section is the central place for finding out what is new on the site. All the news and group-related postings are done here. Since it is a page that represents the total picture of the community, it is known as the community portal. You can post news and notices, view the to-do list, read general guidelines for contributing to the site, view user guides for writing articles, resources, etc. The Wikipedia community portal section looks like this:

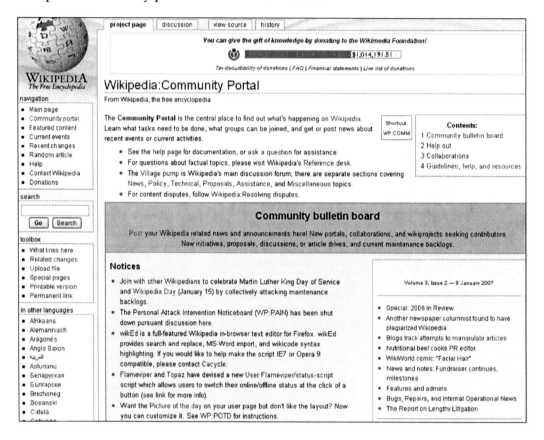

Current Events

The **Current events** link takes you to a page of the site where you can view all the current events. Current events are basically the calendar events that take place both on site and off site. A good example of an on-site current event could be looking for a contributor for ghost articles for the current month. But if you want to list the events that have taken place today in different places, you can do that as well. In order to put something on the current events section, make sure that the event goes with the current calendar. Neither a month-old event nor a future event should be listed in the current events section. This is how a current events section looks like:

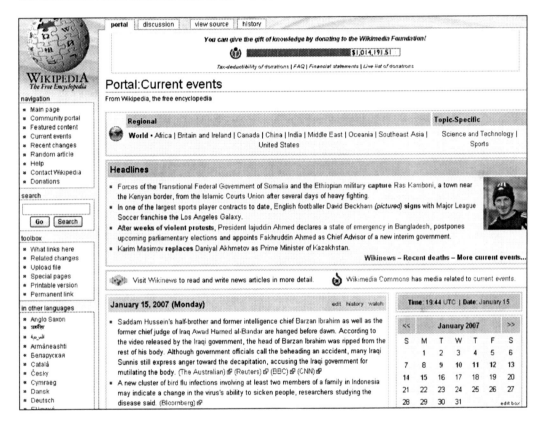

Recent Changes

The **Recent changes** link shows the most recent edits made to the pages in your site. Using this page, you can monitor articles, correct mistakes, and also check for vandalism by unethical users. This link is available at the top and in the sidebar of each page. This link is also the first **special page** in the MediaWiki software. We will learn more about special pages later in this book. The section looks like this:

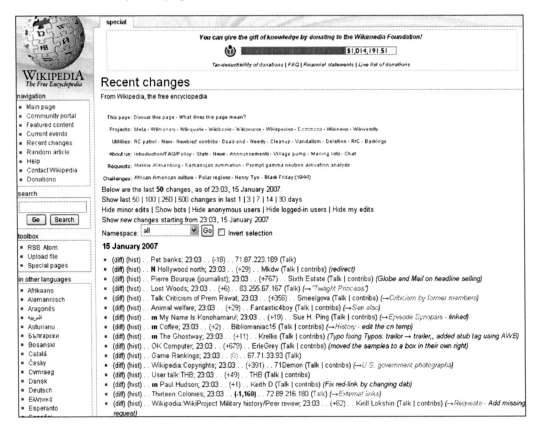

Random Page

As the name suggests, this link will take you to a page that has been chosen by the system randomly. Next time you click the link you won't see the same page again since it will be a new page. Basically it is a special page that is used for taking users to a random page within the wiki.

Search

The box below the navigation section is the search area. You can search for a page within the wiki using the **Search** button The **Go** button is used to quickly jump to a page, if the title is known to you. **Search** is a powerful tool to find an existing or similar article. If an exact match of the search phrase is found in the wiki, then you will be directed to the exact match page. If the search phrase is found in any article then search result will be shown with relevancy of the page with the search phrase. For example if you search for a topic called "ghost" in Wikipedia, you will be taken to a page named ghost. But if you search "ghost type" then you will see the following page:

Toolbox

Just below the search section is the **toolbox** section. This section is very helpful once you are familiar with MediaWiki. We have some very useful links in the toolbox section such as **What links here, Related changes, Special pages, Upload file**, etc. So let's quickly summarize these features:

- **What links here**: This is a special page where you can find the names of all the pages that link to the current page. These are also known as **backlinks**. This link helps us to find a related article, broken links, and double redirection of the links.

- **Related changes**: This feature lists the recent changes made in every article that is linked from the current page, but not more than the number specified in the preferences. This is a modified version of recent changes that is limited to a specified number.

- **Special pages**: These pages do not have any corresponding wiki text, which means that users cannot make any changes to the functionality of the pages. It is build by the system on demand. We will learn more about these features in Chapter 5.

- **Upload file**: The **Upload file** link will take you to a section of the site where you can upload permitted file types to the wiki site. This link is shown based on the setup of wiki site, which describes who can upload and which file types can be uploaded. We will have a detailed discussion in the next chapter on file upload.

Login Section

The top right side of the page is the user section where you can see a message **Log in/create account**. When you create an account or log in you will see this text message is gone and there are few links instead. Also when you log in the number of body section tabs also increases. Those links are basically for registered users and based on the setup of the site. As we dig more, we will get used to these terms more easily.

            Log in / create account

Main Body Section

The fourth section of the page is the main body section. This body section can also be divided into a few parts. As you look at the page, you will see a few tabs at the top of the body box. These tabs are used for different purposes. They are **article, discussion, edit**, and **history**. Below the tabs, the title section provides the page title.

Below the title and the horizontal line is the main body section of the page. This is the section that will be created or modified by users.

Footer

The bottom part of the page contains the footer section, which holds information about the site, along with MediaWiki images and a disclaimer. We can also format that for our purpose (we will learn more of these formatting techniques later on in this book).

Now let's learn how to create a page.

Creating New Pages for the Haunted

There are various ways in which you can create a page; a few of them are:

Creating a New Page Using a Link from an Existing Page

Now that we have a good idea about the MediaWiki software and its navigation system, let's create our first page for the haunted site. There are a lot of ways of creating pages in MediaWiki and some of them are as easy as clicking a button.

Let's say we want to create a new page named **Welcome**. In order to do so, remove all the text in the textbox and add the following text in the box and save it by clicking the **Save page** button.

```
[[Welcome]] to the haunted site.
```

What we are doing here is creating a link from the main page to a new page named **Welcome** (here [[welcome]] indicates the new page). Don't worry about the syntax now. We will talk about syntax later in this chapter and also in the next chapter.

If you want to see the preview of the page before saving it, then click the **Show preview** button. You can also see the changes made by you in the current page by clicking the **Show changes** button. We will have a detailed discussion about these buttons later in this chapter. When we save the page, it will be loaded in a window with the **Welcome** text marked as a link. Follow the link and you will be taken to the not existent page named **Welcome**. Since this page does not exist, it will be opened in editing mode and a message will be shown at the top of the editing section. The message will be similar to this:

You've followed a link to a page that doesn't exist yet. To create the page, start typing in the box below (see the help page for more info). If you are here by mistake, just click your browser's back button.

Warning: You are not logged in. Your IP address will be recorded in this page's edit history.

Now type in the text. Since this page does not exist, save this page first, else all the changes we have made will be gone. After you click **Save Page**, we are done with creating a new page for the site using MediaWiki.

 **Flying high:** Until now you have heard that a wiki is the simplest tool to create content. Now you can see yourself how simple it is to create a page and link it with other pages. You can create pages and links on the fly using MediaWiki. A content management system is better when you can manage your content more efficiently and create content more easily. If we focus on this point then definitely a wiki is a better choice for us for content management system.

Creating a New Page Using the Search Option

Since a wiki is a collaborative site, there is a good chance that the content you want to add is already there. So, whenever you want to create a new page, it is always safer to perform a search in order to find if the page title has been taken or not. You can perform a search using the search area in the left navigation panel and find out the result. If you click on the **Go** button then it shows the availability of the page. If the page already exists then the search result will show that; otherwise the search result will show you that the page is not found with a link to create the new page. Follow the link and you will be taken to an empty page where you can edit and save it as a new page.

Creating a New Page through the URL

We will use a hack in order to create a new page in MediaWiki. Suppose we want to create a page named **Welcome** for our haunted site. Let's do the following step and see how easily we can create the new page. Remember, when we were in the main page, the title of the main page was (it's just an example site address):

```
http://www.haunted.com/index.php?title=Main_Page
```

 If you have PHP installed as an Apache module, then the URL notation used would be: `http://www.haunted.com/index.php/Main_Page`.

Now remove the Main_Page word and add our desired page title **Welcome** and press *Enter* to load the page and voilà, we are done. The new page comes with the title we provided in the URL. Now click **edit** and enter some text and save the page. For example in order to create a new page on our site named Ghost Stories, we have to write the following URL:

```
http://www.haunted.com/index.php?title=Ghost Stories
```

Considerations before Adding a New Page/New Content

We have seen the ways in which we can create new pages using MediaWiki. Since we have more than one option to create a new page, it is always confusing to choose which approach is better suited to our needs. If our site is a searchable reference-type site, then adding by search method is more suitable. If we want to get new content for a page that we do not have yet, then we can find some similar contents and put the links on those similar content pages. Then enthusiast visitors can add content to it. Whichever approach we choose for our solution, we must remember a few things before creating a new page:

- It is a good approach to search for the page before creating a new page. In an ideal scenario a wiki site will contain lots of pages and the prior existence of the page that you are thinking is not impossible here. So first look for similar types of pages in the system. If it does not exist then you can create it, but if it exists then you can do two things. Either you can append changes to the existing page, or you can make a new page with a new title, so that it does not conflict with other pages. While appending an existing page, it is always important to go through the editing guidelines provided by the site or consider the existing content and approaches.

- It is always recommended to review the changes you make before saving them. We must follow a good naming convention for the page. We will discuss more about page naming later in this chapter. You can review it with the **Show changes** button, which will give you the exact scenario of what you have changed, and you can always undo your changes if required.

- Before saving a page we must check for the links bound to that page. We can do this by using the **What links here** option. We can add links or modify them from this option for the newly added page. If the page is isolated, meaning that we did not create any inbound and outbound links, then make sure that other pages have some link with it, or else it will be just an orphan page. In order to avoid such scenarios it is best to add pages by linking.

 Creating a blank page: Creating a new page and a blank page might sound similar, but there are technical differences. The blank page in MediaWiki has page history, but for the new page, page history is not available.

Page Name Convention

As we have seen, the page name we provide becomes the title of the page or vice versa. So it is vital to have a very good and meaningful page name for any page. There are some rules regarding the page naming in MediaWiki. Here are a few:

- **Use valid characters**: Page names or titles cannot have special characters (such as [,], {, }, |, #, <, and >) that are used by MediaWiki internally. MediaWiki processes wiki syntax before formatting; so anything used by MediaWiki will be converted and executed before the formatting of the text. [,], {, }, |, and # characters are used for linking in a wiki. So we must be careful about using special characters. Also do not use any non-printable character such as the *Delete* key.

> Valid characters for a page title are: A-Z, 0-9, %, /, ?, :, @, =, &, $, _, -, +, !, *, ', (,), and , .
>
> Note: you can define the valid title characters in MediaWiki. In the DefaultSettings.php file under the includes folder, we have one variable $wgLegalTitleChars. This variable defines which characters are allowed as legal title characters. You can redefine the variable in LocalSettings.php file in order to redefine the legal character list. We will learn more about configuration issues at the end of the book.

One interesting thing in the valid character set is the forward slash (/). It is a valid character used in a URL but it has a very special meaning. The forward slash is used to indicate sub-pages for a page. If sub-pages are activated in the wiki, then forward slash is used to indicate sub-pages. So it is not recommended to use this in a page title when sub-pages are active. We will learn more about sub-pages later in the book.

- **Do not use a namespace as a name**: All the pages created using MediaWiki belong to a **namespace**. The namespace term is used to separate contents into different levels based on policy and discussion. The core intention of using namespaces is separating contents. They encourage separation of the pages of a wiki into a core set intended for public viewing and private information intended for the editing community and restricted access. When you do not provide any namespace before a page title, it defaults to the main namespace. For example, http://en.wikipedia.org/wiki/Main_Page is a page in the Main Namespace whereas http://en.wikipedia.org/wiki/Wikipedia:Featured_articles is a page in the Project Namespace. We will learn more about namespaces in the coming chapters.

So we should remember that a page name cannot start with a prefix that is used to refer another project or one of the **pseudo-namespaces** Media: and Special:. Pseudo-namespaces are not actual namespaces in a wiki. They provide a shortcut for the frequently visited pages in a wiki. For example Media: is pseudo-namespace for images and other files.

- **Do not use a very long page title:** Always try to restrict the length of the page title to be not more than 255 characters. If the title length is more than this, then it will be automatically truncated. This is valid for all ASCII characters. But if your title consists of non-ASCII characters, then each non-ASCII character in UTF-8 encoding can take up to 4 bytes of space, which means you will have less than 255 characters in the title. In ASCII character each character takes 1 byte, so we can have maximum 255 characters if we are using ASCII characters.

 Character coding in the URL does not take more than one space. So an entry of %3B in the URL will not count as 3 characters but as the single character that it represents, which is a semicolon (;).

Formatting Pages

An important aspect of building pages is to format the pages to make them more structured to view. We can format our pages using the editor option in the edit page or we can use wiki syntax directly in the edit panel.

Wiki syntax is a special set of markup characters that is used by MediaWiki for formatting content. As we know, to show our contents in web page we use HTML tags for formatting. MediaWiki itself is a web-based site, but it still has its own syntax and markup rules. During the rendering of the page MediaWiki converts their markup syntax into corresponding HTML syntax. So as a user we don't have to know all the HTML tags to edit any pages. The wiki syntax gives the flexibility to format the content with very easy-to-use steps. The following chart shows the basic difference between general text, HTML, and wiki syntax.

Expected Output	HTML	MediaWiki
Welcome to **Haunted**. The place for ghost hunters all around the world. Our mission is	Welcome to \<strong> Haunted\</strong>. The place for ghost hunters all around the world. Our mission is \ 	Welcome to "Haunted" The place for ghost hunters all around the world. Our mission is
• centralize all information about ghost	\<ul>	* centralize all information about ghost
• share our stories, ideas and images	\<li> centralize all information about ghost	* share our stories, ideas and images
• exploring new haunted places	\<li>share our stories, ideas and images	* exploring new haunted places
Click here to learn more.	\<li>exploring new haunted places	[[Click here]] to learn more.
	\</ul>	
	\ 	
	\<a href="learnmore. html">Click here\</a> to learn more.	

So we can see a clear difference between HTML and wiki markups. It is obvious that wiki markups are easy to learn and easy to apply. The wiki markups themselves are user friendly. Anyone without any knowledge of HTML tags can create or edit pages with a little knowledge about wiki syntax.

Click the **edit** link of the page you are in and that will take you to the edit section. There under the title **Editing Main Page** (for example) you will see an editing section where you can type. Just above that there are few buttons placed to help you during editing.

The editor we have seen is not an editor of the What You See Is What You Get or WYSIWYG type. In WYSIWYG, whatever you see during editing will be shown exactly in the browser, after saving. In general this type of editor lets you work on the final output directly rather than working with tags and syntax. The philosophy of WYSIWYG is you design and I will build. But for this editor, which is not a WYSIWYG editor, we have to design and build the code. So let's explore what functionality the wiki editor does provide us.

Icon	Function	Corresponding Wiki syntax
B	To emphasize the text with bold.	'''your bold text'''
I	To emphasize the text as italics.	''your italic text''
Ab	Create Links to an internal page.	[[wiki page]]
	Link to a page in the Web.	[www.packtpub.com]
A	Text formatting for Headings 2.	= = Heading two = =
	Adds an image to the page. Here it is assumed that the image is located in the site.	[[Image:Example.jpg]]
	This button links to previously loaded media files such as audio and video.	[[Media:Example.mp3]]
√n	Insert mathematical formulas in the page.	\<math\>Insert formula here\</math\>
W	This button gives the option of not rendering any text according to wiki syntax in the page. So you can select any text and mark it as non-wiki text, which will be ignored during page rendering by MediaWiki.	\<nowiki\>Insert non-formatted text here\</nowiki\>
	This function inserts your IP address or user name and time stamp based on your login to the page. This helps to show the contributors to a page.	--~~~~
	This button inserts a horizontal line in your page.	----

So this is the formatting we can do using the buttons provided in the edit panel. But these are not the only formatting options available in MediaWiki. The formatting options in MediaWiki are vast and there are so many things to use. So let's discuss formatting options in MediaWiki

Formatting Text

As we have seen in the editing bar, two apostrophes on each side of the text will make your text italics and three apostrophes on each side will make your text bold; five apostrophes on both sides will make the text bold and italics.

Here is an example of how you use this feature.

Let's write the following content in the edit box:

```
Welcome to the most '''haunted''' place in the ''internet''.
You will get all information about exploring haunted places
all around the globe. We have '''''pictures''''', '''''video
clips''''' , '''''real stories''''', '''''location and description
of haunted place''''' and last but not least the '''''ghost
hunters''''', who dare to explore the unthinkable.
```

And you will see the following output after saving the page:

Adding a Line Break

To make our content look structured, we create paragraphs for similar content. In order to separate the lines, we need to put a line break between them. There are two ways to create line breaks:

- Pressing the *Enter* key takes the cursor to the next line, but after saving the page it is merged with the previous paragraph. To avoid this press *Enter* key twice to insert a blank line between two lines or paragraphs.

- The second option is to use HTML line break tag `<br>` to indicate a line break. We will discuss HTML support in formatting wiki content later in the chapter.

Type the following in the edit box and add one blank line between the lines where you want line breaks:

```
If you are interested to contribute to this site then you are always
welcome to do that by contributing to the following options:

Providing information about haunted site

Writing articles and stories both real and imaginative

Adding images to our image gallery

By letting other know about our site.
```

Now save the page and review it in the browser. The following screen is observed:

Section and Subsection Creation

Headings are used to organize the sections and subsections in the content area. MediaWiki supports three types of headings:

- Heading 2 with two equal signs (= =) at the beginning and end of the text
- Heading 3 with three equal signs (= = =) at the beginning and end of the text
- Heading 4 with four equal signs (= = = =) at the beginning and end of the text

It is also interesting to know that if an article has more than four headings, a Table of Contents is automatically created based on the headings; so it is very important to know how to apply the headings. We will see an example of a Table of Contents after the following example:

> Do not use Heading 1 (single = sign) because it gives the article title and there should not be two titles for a single article. That's why the sub-section concept is used. To write in a proper way, always start from two equal signs. Also do not skip sub-sections such as Heading 2 followed by Heading 4, or there will be a problem during the creation of the Table of Contents.

For an example, write down the following in the edit box:

```
Here is the list of haunted places around the world
==Haunted places in America==
===Haunted places in New York===
====Haunted places in Brooklyn====
====Haunted places in Long Island====
===Haunted places in Florida===
===Haunted places in Boston===
==Haunted places in Europe==
===Haunted places in United Kingdom===
====Haunted places in London====
===Haunted places in Ireland===
===Haunted places in Australia===
===Haunted places in Africa===
===Haunted places in Asia===
====Haunted places in Himalayas====
```

Save the page. You will see the following image:

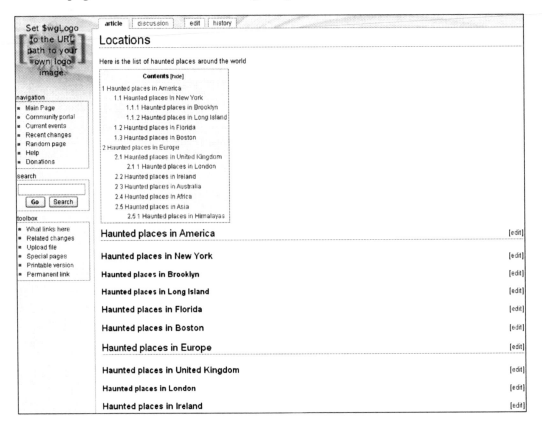

In the previous figure the **Contents** section is also known as the Table of Contents. We will learn more about the Table of Contents and its customization in the next chapter.

Indentation and Signature

Formatting text or paragraphs requires indentation, especially when the content is large. In MediaWiki we can indent a line or paragraph by starting it with a colon (:). For every colon we provide at the beginning of the line, we get more indentation.

Write the following example in the edit box:

```
First Ghost Hunting Camp by NewYork Haunted Group - 2 days at Ohio,
USA

Day 1 : Starting From NewYork - Ohio

:Morning
:: 10:00 AM Gather at City Hall
:: 10:15 AM Briefing to the Team
:: 10:30 AM Start for the Airport


:Afternoon
:: 01:00 PM Check In to Hotel in Ohio
:: 01:30 PM Lunch at Hotel and rest
:: 05:30 PM Start Preparing for the Haunting Night
:: 06:30 PM Team Briefing
:Night
:: 07:00 PM Reaching the Spot and start hunting
:: 03:30 AM Meeting at the Common Place
:: 04:30 AM Return to Hotel


Day 2 : Returning from Ohio - NewYork

:Morning
:: 10:30 AM Gather in Hotel Lobby
:: 11:30 AM Arrive at the Airport
:: 11:45 AM On Board
:Afternoon
:: 01:00 PM Land at NY
:: 02:30 PM Gather at City Hall
:: 03:00 PM Team experience and Presentation Start
::: Presentation :
::::Team 1
::::Team 2
::::Team 3
:::Choosing Most Active Member of the Tour
:::Awarding the best Ghost Hunter
:: 05:30 PM Concluding Speech
```

Save the page. You will see the following page:

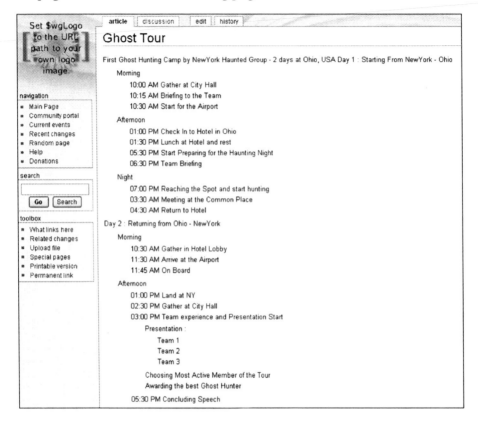

Now let's talk about signing a page. When you add comments in a talk page or in any discussion, it is a good practice to sign your name. This option makes others aware about the username, date, time, and the content edited. For formatting remember the following simple rules:

To add your user name use three tildes	~~~
To add your user name and date/time use four tildes	~~~~
To add only date/time use five tildes	~~~~~

Try out the following example:

```
User :
: ~~~
User name & date/time:
: ~~~~
Date/time:
: ~~~~~
```

The following output is observed:

Set $wgLogo to the URL path to your own logo image.	**article** discussion edit history
	Tour Comments
navigation	User :
• Main Page	127.0.0.1
• Community portal	User name & date/time:
• Current events	127.0.0.1 05:29, 16 January 2007 (Central Asia Standard Time)
• Recent changes	Date/time:
• Random page	05:29, 16 January 2007 (Central Asia Standard Time)
• Help	
• Donations	This page was last modified 23:29, 15 January 2007. Privacy policy About Haunted Disclaimers

> You may notice that an IP address is shown instead of a user name; this is because unregistered users do not have a user name and are identified by their IP address.

Now we will focus more on tag-based (<>) formatting. These tags are used in wiki markup as well as HTML. The coming sections will explore more about the usage of HTML tags in our wiki site.

Using HTML Tags for Formatting

In the last few years HTML-based emails, messages, and newsletters have become so popular that many online content editing software applications allow tags to be incorporated with text in the edit box. MediaWiki is no exception, but unlike others, MediaWiki restricts use of certain HTML tags in its edit section. We can only use the set of tags permitted by MediaWiki. We can also allow all HTML tags to be incorporated with MediaWiki, but it is not advisable to do so in a public domain and is also not secure to allow all raw HTML. We can restrict such raw HTML input for permitted user groups in our site but we will learn more about this in the Administration chapter of the book.

The list of tags supported by the MediaWiki engine is:

`<b>`	`<h2>`	`<s>`
`<big>`	`<h3>`	`<small>`
`<blockquote>`	`<h4>`	`<strike>`
` `	`<h5>`	`<strong>`
`<caption>`	`<h6>`	`<sub>`
`<center>`	`<hr>`	`<sup>`
`<cite>`	`<i>`	`<table>`
`<code>`	`<li>`	`<td>`
`<dd>`	`<ol>`	`<th>`
`<div>`	`<p>`	`<tr>`
`<dl>`	`<pre>`	`<tt>`
`<dt>`	`<rb>`	`<u>`
`<em>`	`<rp>`	`<ul>`
`<font>`	`<rt>`	`<var>`
`<h1>`	`<ruby>`	`<!-- ... -->`

So any tag outside this list will not be rendered properly by the wiki engine. For example the image tag `<img>` is not supported by the wiki engine. So when we try to add an image tag like:

```
<img src="haunted.gif" border=0 alt="Haunted logo">
```

We will not get our desired result here. The output will be as shown in the following figure:

We can add images to MediaWiki and we will see that in the next chapter. Like the `<img>` tag, the anchor tag `<a>` is also not supported in MediaWiki. It is also important to note that there are few tags that can be **nested** inside the wiki text. So we can use nested tags for better formatting, especially for pages with tables and lists. The supported nested tags in MediaWiki are:

`<table>`	`< blockquote >`	`<big>`
`<td>`	`<ol>`	`<small>`
`<th>`	`<ul>`	`<sub>`
`<tr>`	`<dl>`	`<sup>`
`<div>`	`<font>`	

As we know, each HTML tag has some attributes, and we can set attributes' values to customize the tags for our purpose. So it is necessary for any software to set attribute options for HTML tags. MediaWiki has this option for a limited range of attributes.

The attributes supported by MediaWiki are:

title	align	lang	dir
width	height	bgcolor	clear
noshade	cite	size	face
color	type	start	value
compact	summary		border
frame	rules	cellspacing	cellpadding
valign	char	charoff	colgroup
col	span	abbr	axis
headers	scope	rowspan	colspan
id	class	name	style

In the following example we can use HTML in our wiki edit option. We will use both HTML and wiki syntax:

```
Let's share a story about a <b>Ghost</b> in a small village near
'''Michigan'''

<h2><center>A story of the '''''Crying Girl''''' </center></h2>

::The village name is known as <tt>ghost village</tt>. People used
to say there is a ghost near the river bank which comes out
after every midnight. Some people have reported seeing her.

<code><span style="font-variant:small-caps">
"She is around 14 years old. She always wears a white dress and
she holds a little doll in her hand."
</span>
</code>

<span>
.. says a person from the village who claims to have seen the little
girl a few times
</span>

<i>It is said that the girl drowned in the river long time
ago while crossing the river by boat with family members.
Everyone in the boat died. The girl also lost her younger
brother in this accident. His body was never found. That's
why she comes out every night to find her lost
brother.</i><br>
```

The following output is produced:

The previous example shows that we can easily integrate HTML and wiki syntax, or use only HTML tags to create pages. We will learn more about HTML tags and attributes in the next chapter when we discuss advance formatting techniques.

Show Things as they Are

Sometimes it is necessary to show some content without any formatting. For example, any double-quoted text will be changed to italics by the wiki engine. In order to show the quotes around the text, the no formatting option is used. You might require the HTML code to give people the link code to your site. For such issues we need to show the content as it is without any formatting. There are few ways to do this. We will explore how we can show the contents as it is written in the edit box.

We can use these non-formatting techniques when we need to show something such as formulas, equations, ASCII images, a code section, etc.

The `<nowiki>` tag is used for non-formatting wiki syntax. If we use `<nowiki>` and `</nowiki>` tags before and at the end of the text block, then the wiki engine will ignore all the wiki syntax inside the text block as well as the HTML codes. However it reformats the text and removes new lines and multiple spaces from the text. It also interprets special characters and character coding.

```
In order to Put a Link of our site on your site, copy paste the
following line to your site pages:
<nowiki>
<a herf="http://www.haunted.com"> Haunted    -   The place for Ghost
enthusiast </a>
</nowiki>
```

The following output is produced:

Another tag that provides a no formatting option is the `<pre>` tag of HTML. The `<pre>` tag ignores wiki markup and also HTML markup. It also shows special characters and character encoding. However, unlike `<nowiki>`, the `<pre>` tag does not reformat text. So, new lines and spaces will not be removed. Here is the example shown above but with the `<pre>` tag.

```
In order to Put a Link of our site on your site, copy paste the
following line to your site pages:
<pre>
<a herf="http://www.haunted.com"> Haunted    -   The place for Ghost
enthusiast </a>
</pre>
```

The output will be:

Notice the difference between the nowiki and pre output. The spaces around the hyphen are omitted in nowiki but in the `<pre>` tag they are kept as they are.

Another technique to preserve formatting is through application of leading spaces. The text is not reformatted if a space is inserted at the beginning of each line. This technique will interpret wiki syntax and HTML markups but will not reformat the text. It also shows special characters and character coding.

```
In order to Put a Link of our site on your site, copy paste the
following line to your site pages:
<a herf="http://www.haunted.com"> Haunted    -    The place
for Ghost enthusiast </a>
```

The following output is observed:

Creating Links and References

As we create new pages, it is necessary to build a relationship among pages. We can do this by creating links between pages.

The three types of hyperlinks available in MediaWiki are:

- Internal link
- Interwiki link
- External link

Internal links are valid inside the installed wiki. All pages referenced by these links lie within the domain of your project or installation, whereas interwiki linking is between two different wikis (sister projects). External links are links made to the outside Web using protocols such as HTTP, FTP, etc.

Creating Internal Links

Creating an internal link in MediaWiki is easier than the other methods listed previously. Just put two brackets at the beginning and end of the link text and we are done. So if we want to create a link to a page named "Story page", then we would write it as `[[Story page]]`. After saving, **Story page** will be shown as a link, and on clicking, we will be taken to the linked page if it exists. If the page doesn't exist then this will take us to the **Editing Story** page. This is the way in which we earlier created a new page.

Self linking: A self link is a link to the page itself. It appears as bold text when the article is viewed. For example if you are on the main page and you want to create a link to the main page, then it is known as self linking.

Indirect self link: An indirect self link is a link to a page that redirects back to the original page. Say you are on page A and you link to page B but page B redirects you to page A. In this case the self-link feature does not work, even though the feature would be equally useful here. Also, when the prefix for the project itself is added (interwiki-link style, but again linking to the page itself) the self-link feature does not work. Self linking is used specially on navigating templates. Suppose we have a menu of 5 links and each link takes you to a page. For example we can have five menu links A, B, C, D, E and these links are common to all five pages. When you are visiting any page A, B, C, D, or E, the link is also there. So when you are on page B, the link for page B will be a self link for that page, and it will be shown as bold and be non-clickable. But when you are on a page other than B, you can click on that link. This is true for all pages. We will learn about templates later in this book.

Creating Interwiki Links

Using interwiki links, we can create links to other sites on the Internet. This gives users the option to avoid pasting in entire URLs (as for regular web pages) and instead use shorthand by adding a prefix to another wiki. For example, `[[wikipedia:interWiki]]` links to the wikipedia:interWiki article on the English Wikipedia. For each project we can specify an interwiki map, which is a list of target projects with their prefixes. Interwiki links are created by Administrators. We will learn more about how to create this interwiki mapping in Chapter 7. Since wiki projects are not listed like domain names, it is the responsibility of the site owner or project creator to define the wiki map to its server. Without a mapping the interwiki feature will not work. The best feature about interwiki linking is that these target projects need not use MediaWiki and need not even be a wiki.

Uses of Interwiki Linking

Let's say that our haunted site is getting popular all over the world and people want to create their own haunted sites on a country basis. Now if 20 countries have 20 different haunted sites based on wikis, then the best way to connect them together would be by using interwiki linking. Also, if we have a language-supported site that supports different languages you can think of each language as a site so that supporting languages can also be done using interwiki linking.

A site's own namespace prefix cannot be reused as prefix code for an external site/project. However, the prefix used for a target site/ project may be the same as the prefix for a project namespace within that project. As a result, to link to a page in the target namespace, just use the same prefix twice. Suppose our haunted site in America has a namespace called story and our own new wiki site also has a namespace by the same name. To link our namespace to the story namespace of the American haunted site we need to need to write the link as [[story:story:new story]].

External Linking

External linking is used to link to a page on the World Wide Web. A single pair of brackets [ ] is used to indicate external linking. A valid external link will be written as [http://www.packtpub.com], which will create a link to Packt Publishing's website. The interesting thing about external linking is that if you write the wiki link as [http://www.packtpub.com], then it will show up as a number on the screen. Let us see this with an example:

```
[http://www.packtpub.com]

[http://en.wikipedia.org/wiki/List_of_haunted_locations]

[http://www.Dracula.com]

[http://www.vampire.com]

[http://www.witch.com]

[http://en.wikipedia.org/wiki/Ghost_Hunters]
```

The output for this is shown here:

As you can see, the links are shown as numbers on screen. We should name these links so that the reader sees some text rather than numbers on the screen. We will learn this technique in the next section.

Now let's have a look at the protocols that are supported by MediaWiki. External linking works with the following protocols:

- HTTP
- HTTPS
- FTP
- Gopher
- NEWS
- mailto
- IRC

If you want to add other types of protocols such as `files://`, then you have to modify the `LocalSettings.php` file under the root folder. We will learn these techniques along with others in Chapter 7.

We have already learned about creating links from MediaWiki but we still haven't discussed creating links to a subsection of a page or naming links so that the link shows up as a label instead of a number in the view page. We will discuss these things now.

Anchoring

Creating a link within the same page is called anchoring. Suppose we are in a page where we have lots of subsections and there is a link to each subsection in the table of contents. When we click on the link for the subsection, the page automatically scrolls down to that section. This is known as anchoring. It is possible to link to a specific portion of a page with the help of anchors.

HTML headers or wiki sections and subsections automatically become HTML anchors, which can be linked to. Also `id` attributes of HTML tags in the wiki can be used as anchors. Such items as `<div id="ghostOne">` Information of First ghost `</div>` can be anchored no matter wherever this text exists in the page.

To refer to an anchor, include the hash sign (#) and the header name or the `id` tag name inside a regular wiki link, like `[[page#anchor_name]]`.

So let's create some links and see how it looks on the main page.

```
For Wiki books: [http://www.packtpub.com]

Haunted location:
[http://en.wikipedia.org/wiki/List_of_haunted_locations#United_States]

Dracula: [http://www.Dracula.com]

Vampire: [http://www.vampire.com]

Witch: [http://www.witch.com]

Ghost hunters: [http://en.wikipedia.org/wiki/Ghost_Hunters]
```

The output in the main screen will be seen as follows:

If you now click the **Haunted location** link it will take you to the **Unites States** subsection of the Haunted Location page. The links don't look that good on screen. We can replace the links with text using piped links, which we will cover in the next section.

Piped Links

A piped link is a link within the site or to a sister site that is labeled differently from the name of the page it links to. It can be any text that you want to show in the appearance of the page. This allows linking a word or phrase within the text of a page rather than using the link itself, even if the wording does not exactly correspond with the name of the other page. The term piped refers to the use of the pipe character "|" used to separate the description from the actual link.

The structure of a piped link is like this:

```
[[actual link | Link label]]
```

So the piped link:

`[http://en.wikipedia.org/wiki/List_of_haunted_locations#United_States| Haunted Locations in USA]` will show **Haunted Locations in USA** link on the WikiPedia page where this code is written.

Some rules about piped link creation:

If in a piped link the part following the "|" is left empty, it is converted to an abbreviated form of the page name on the left, as follows:

- If there is a colon in it, the leftmost colon and anything to the left side of it is removed.
- If there is a text in parentheses at the end, it will be removed.
- If there is nothing to abbreviate, there is no colon and there are no parentheses, then the link does not work at all.
- Piped links are created for internal and interwiki links, not for external links.

 For external links, we have to use a space in between the link and description to have the same effect.

So let's change our links to piped links to give them a better look. Enter the following:

```
For Wiki books: [http://www.packtpub.com Packt Publishing - Horror
Books]

Haunted location: [http://en.wikipedia.org/wiki/List_of_haunted_
locations#United_States All the Haunted Places in USA]

Dracula: [http://www.Dracula.com The Dracula online]

Vampire: [http://www.vampire.com Know everything about Vampire]

Witch: [http://www.witch.com Are you Looking for a witch? Click here.]

Ghost hunters: [http://en.wikipedia.org/wiki/Ghost_Hunters We are
looking for Ghost Hunters. You wanna join?]

Trip to Ohio to hunt ghosts: [[Ghost Tour| Get the Tour Plan and
Register for it]]
```

The following output is obtained:

We observe that the page looks much better than before. Remember one thing: since the HTML hyperlink tag <a> does not work in MediaWiki, never create links using it. So can you just create links in the Main Page to all the pages we have created so far in this chapter? You can have a mini wiki site ready then.

So far we have learned how to make text-based links. Now we will learn how to make image-based links, which we use frequently in other sites.

 We can provide the link names without using the pipe character also. In that case, instead of a pipe character we can put a space just after the link URL and specify the link name.

Creating Image Links

Image-based links are frequently used in the Internet. They also make navigation through the pages easier for the end user. Though we have not discussed how to add images to the wiki page, we will now learn how to make an image-based link. In the next chapter we will learn about adding images to the page and creating links with them. The manner in which MediaWiki handles images loaded on its server and those external to it is different.

In order to create an image link based on an external link (the image is stored in a remote location or different server or anywhere on the Web that is external to the wiki) we can write the following code. But before doing that we have to enable the permission to show external images in our wiki by adding the following declaration in LocalSettings.php file:

```
$wgAllowExternalImages = true;
```

Once we have allowed external images to be shown on our wiki page, we can add images as part of the links. Here is an example of our modified recommended sites:

```
For Wiki books: [http://www.packtpub.com  http://www.packtpub.com/
images/PacktLogoSmall.png]

Haunted location: [http://en.wikipedia.org/wiki/List_of_haunted_
locations#United_States| All the Haunted Places in USA]

Dracula: [http://www.Dracula.com| The Dracula online]

Vampire: [http://www.vampire.com| Know everything about Vampire]

Witch: [http://www.witch.com| Are you Looking for a witch? Click
here.]

Ghost hunters: [http://en.wikipedia.org/wiki/Ghost_Hunters| We are
looking for Ghost Hunters. You wanna join?]

Trip to Ohio to hunt ghosts: [[Ghost Tour| Get the Tour Plan and
Register for it]]
```

The following output is obtained:

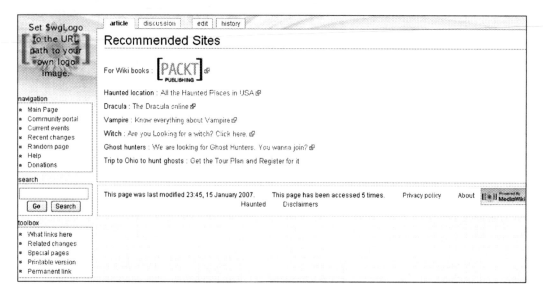

The image of Packt Publishing is shown as link. When we click it we will be taken to the Packt Publishing page. In the next chapter we will learn how to add images without creating links.

Summary

We have learned many things in this chapter, navigating, creating new pages, and also formatting them. We also learned about wiki syntax and how to incorporate HTML with it. In the next chapter we will learn a lot about advanced formatting, designing eyes catching pages as well as organizing contents to make things structured.

4

Advanced Formatting

The image below is that of a new home page for the Ghost site using MediaWiki formatting techniques. However, have we learned these formatting techniques in the previous chapter? No, we have not. In the last chapter, we covered basic formatting. In this chapter we will focus on more advanced formatting. By using advanced formatting, we will be able to create layouts like the image below. Our main focus in this chapter will be on advanced formatting techniques such as tables, lists, images, and advanced HTML.

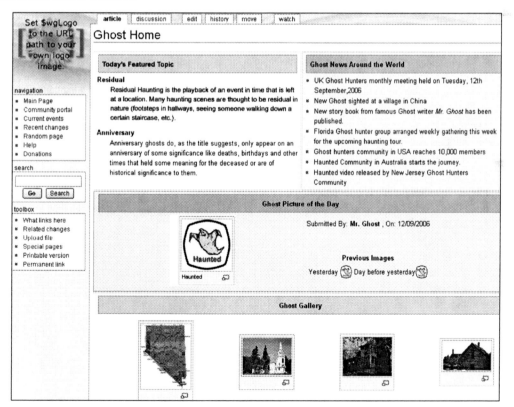

Using Lists with MediaWiki

The three types of lists available in HTML—unordered lists, ordered lists, and definition lists—are also available in MediaWiki. In MediaWiki, we can use both HTML and wiki syntax for creating lists. We will explore both techniques in this chapter.

Unordered List

Creating unordered lists in MediaWiki is very simple. In order to create an unordered list in MediaWiki using wiki syntax, keep the following rules in mind:

- Use the asterisk (*) sign at the beginning of each line for creating a list element. The number of asterisks you add before the line will indicate the level of list element in the unordered list. For example, ** will indicate a second-level list element, while *** will indicate a third-level list element, and so on.

- In order to restart an unordered list, put a wiki line break (an empty line) at the end of the list. Then you can start another list using *.

Let's open a new page and write the following content in order to create an unordered list:

```
* Ghost Directory - North America:
** United States of America.
*** Florida.
*** New York.
**** Long Island
**** Manhattan
**** Cooney Island
*** New Jersey
*** Michigan
* Ghost Directory - Europe:
** United Kingdom
*** Liverpool
*** Fulham
** Ireland
** Finland
** Sweden
Other directories.
* Bangladesh
* India.
```

Now let's click on **Save page** to see the unordered lists that we have created:

Now let us see how to create the same list using HTML syntax:

```
<ul><li>Ghost Directory - North America :
  <ul><li>United States of America.
      <ul><li> Florida.
          <li> New York.
          <ul><li>Long Island
              <li>Manhattan
              <li>Cooney Island
          </ul>
          <li> New Jersey
          <li> Michigan
      </ul>
  </ul>
</ul>
<ul><li> Ghost Directory - Europe:
    <ul><li> United Kingdom
        <ul><li>Liverpool
            <li>Fulham
        </ul>
        <li>Ireland
```

```
            <li>Finland
            <li>Sweden
        </ul>
    </ul>
Other directories.
<ul><li> Bangladesh
        <li> India.
    </ul>
```

From the previous two examples we see that the wiki syntax definitely gives us a less hard time generating the unordered list.

Ordered List

The basic difference between unordered and ordered lists is that while we see only bullets for unordered lists, in an ordered list we will see numbers like 1,2... etc. In order to create an ordered list in MediaWiki using wiki syntax, keep the following rules in mind:

- Use the hash (#) sign for creating each list element. The number of hashes you add before the line will indicate the level of list element in the ordered list. For example, ## will indicate a second-level list element, ### will indicate a third-level list element, and so on.

- In order to restart an ordered list, put a blank line at the end of the list. Then you can then start another list using #.

Now look at the following example in MediaWiki to create an ordered list:

```
In order to submit your story for the Monthly Haunted story contest,
you have to follow the guidelines below:

Stories can have the following Categories
# Novel
# Short Story
# Real life story
# Articles

Here are the writing guidelines
# Basic Guidelines
## Story must be within 1200 words.
## Computer Typed:
### Font size: 12 pt
### Paragraph: double line break
### Font Name: Times New Roman
## Well formatted with a front page
```

```
## Front page content:
### Story name
### Author Name
### Submission Date
### Category
### Author Email Address
# All entries must be submitted before 1st October, 2006
# For any query, contact storyteller@haunted.com
```

Click on **Save page** to see the ordered list, which appears as shown below:

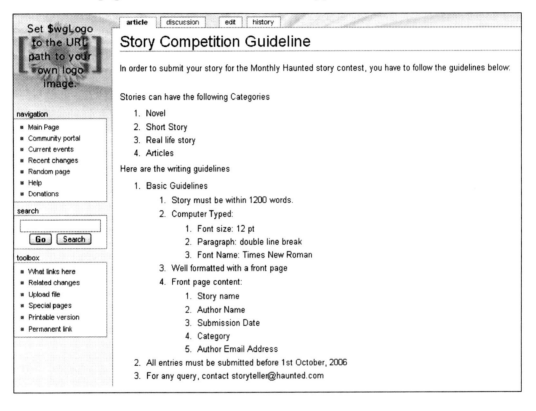

Now if the same example is created with HTML tags, we will see that the wiki syntax is much easier to apply than HTML syntax.

However, there still are some places where we have to use HTML instead of wiki syntax. Take this example: we have a list of ghost sighting for the last 100 years starting from early 1900s. We want to show the sightings sequentially using the years rather than 1, 2, 3, etc. In MediaWiki all ordered lists start from 1, and we cannot define any attribute for wiki syntax. Hence it is not possible for us to start with predefined numbering. Maybe future MediaWiki versions will have something to accommodate this feature.

So let's see how we can perform the task with HTML:

```
Here is the list of ghost sightings in the last 100 years

<ol start=1905>
  <li> Ghosts Sighted in Year 1905
  <ol><li>3rd January: Ghost of ancient Mariner sighted at Port City,
          Florida, USA
      <li> 10th January: Ghost of a Little girl sighted at a village
          in Ireland
      <li> 5th May: A werewolf sighted in a mountain region of
          Colorado.
      <li> 25th December: A Christmas ghost sighted in Texas
  </ol>
  <li> Ghosts Sighted in Year 1906
  <ol><li> 3 sightings have been reported but details about place and
          time are not available.
  </ol>
  <li> Ghosts Sighted in Year 1907
  <ol><li>3rd January: Ghost of ancient Mariner sighted again after
          2 years at Port City, Florida, USA
      <li> 11th June: Ghost of a Mathematician sighted at an old
          valley, Texas
  </ol>
</ol>

<ol start=1937>
  <li> Ghosts Sighted in Year 1937
  <ol><li> January, First Vampire existence found in United Kingdom
      <li> April, A sailor ghost was sighted on a ship bound to
          USA from UK
      <li> July, The sailor ghost again sighted on a ship bound to
          USA from UK - it was named Atlantic Nightmare.
  </ol>
</ol>
```

Click on **Save page** to see the output as shown in the following screenshot:

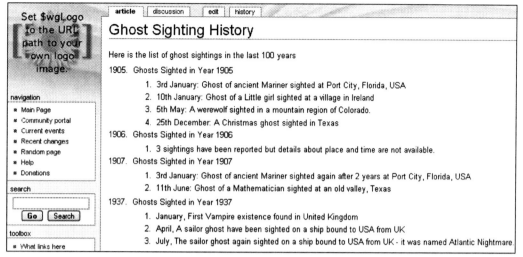

So, from the previous example, we see that it's better to use HTML tags in special cases, where wiki syntax is not of much help. This is the reason why MediaWiki allows the use of HTML tags for formatting.

Definition List

As the name suggests, a definition list contains a glossary-type listing. A definition list is a list of terms and corresponding definitions. Definition lists are typically formatted with the terms on the left, with the definitions following on the right or on the next line. The rules to be kept in mind for creating a definition list are as follows:

- Each definition term should start on a new line.
- To indicate a definition term, use a semi colon (;) at the beginning of the line.
- To indicate the definition, use a colon (:) at the beginning of the definition text.

Let us try an example for definition list creation using wiki syntax:

```
;Residual
:Residual Haunting is the playback of an event in time that is left
at a location. Many haunting scenes are thought to be residual in
nature (footsteps in hallways, seeing someone walking down a certain
staircase, etc.). They are endless loops of the same scene being
played over and over, and they are usually always experienced in the
same location.
```

```
;Anniversary
:Anniversary ghosts do, as the title suggests, only appear on an
anniversary of some significance like deaths, birthdays and other
times that held some meaning for the deceased or are of historical
significance to them. Since this type of ghost only appears on the
anniversary of a special event, it seems likely this type of haunting
could be a residual haunting, reenacting a certain event in time on
that one day or night.

;Intelligent: Unlike residual haunting, ghosts of this type are
not in a 'stuck in time' type of deal. They actually seem to have
intelligence. These spirits are interactive, sometimes verging into
the territory of the poltergeist. They may try and attract your
attention by creating odors, moving things, making noises such as
footsteps, slamming doors, or moving and hiding objects.

;Poltergeist:The Poltergeist - German for "noisy spirit" - seems
to be between the categories of ghost and psi (the term applied to
unusual abilities of human origin such as ESP and psycho kinesis and
investigating "exceptional human experiences" such as out of body
and apparitional experiences). There are usually two camps of thought
on this subject. Some believe it all to be caused by intelligent
ghosts, and some believe it all to be caused by the living person at
the location.
```

The output of the previous example will be as shown in the following screenshot:

According to our discussion so far, we have learned that in order to restart the numbering for an ordered list, or to create a new unordered list, we have to enter a line break. But what if we need to put a break in the text in the list item itself? For unordered list, the bullet item will be shown just below the line break without any notification. However, the problem will be for ordered lists since after every line break the numbering will resume from 1. Unfortunately, wiki syntax cannot help us to solve the problem here. We have to use an HTML solution for this. There are two options available for our rescue:

- Using
- Using <p></p>

Now we will explore a mixture of ordered, unordered, and definition lists in a single example. Here is one demonstration of achieving the task using wiki syntax along with HTML tags:

```
; Ghosts: Ghosts are controversial phenomena that many believe in and
many don't.
* Ghost Directory - North America
  <p> this list includes all haunted places in the North America
      region by country, state and city. We tried to make the
      navigation easier with the use of proper listing.
  </p>
# United States of America.
## Florida.
## New York.
### Long Island<p> Maximum ghosts were found here.</p>Mostly in the
early 1990s.
### Manhattan
### Coney Island
## New Jersey
## Michigan
* Ghost Directory - Europe: we have lots of haunted places in Europe.
<br> Here are few of the places
# United Kingdom
## Liverpool
## Fulham
# Ireland
# Finland
# Sweden
Other directories: <br><br> our other directories include countries
from South Asia and the Middle East.
* Bangladesh
* India.
```

The output appears like the following screenshot:

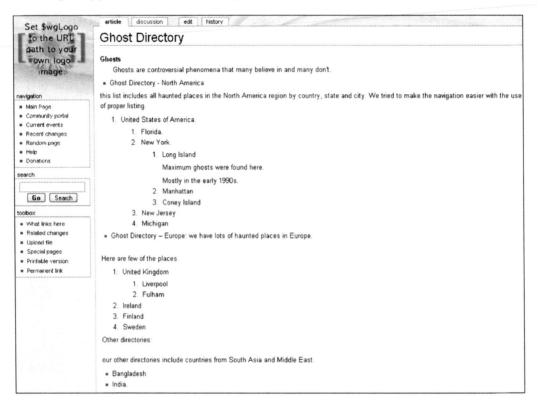

Using Tables

Tables are a very important formatting tool for web applications. Using tables we can create attractive designs and also organize our text and contents. Without tables, lots of things are not possible in HTML, especially advanced formatting. Even for the wiki, we need tables to format our text and images and present our content to the browser. Wiki syntax provides us the opportunity to create tables. Though the syntax is not very conventional it is still very easy to apply.

The Syntax

To create a table in MediaWiki, we need to use curly braces and a vertical line like {| |}. {| is used to open the table and |} to close the table. All the table contents will be between these two tags. This is also known as **wiki-pipe** syntax.

Note: both opening and closing table syntax must reside on a separate line. No other tags apart from attributes of the tables may exist in those two lines; else the table will not be rendered properly.

A few things that we must know before creating a table using wiki syntax are:

- To start a table row enter a line and a dash | - after the opening tag. There is no end symbol for indicating row end. We have to start a new row to add the next line of text or symbols.

 Just like the table opening and closing tags, we cannot put any other characters or symbols on the row indicating line.

- To start a column put a line (|) followed by data or content after the row syntax. If we want to put more than one column of data in a single line, then we have to use (||) instead of (|). The default syntax will have one line (|).

- Each row must have same number of cells as in other rows, so that the number of columns in the table is kept constant. This rule can have an exception if the table cells span multiple rows or columns. If we have any blank cell we must put a non-breaking space ( ) in it so that the cell is displayed. If this rule is broken, the table will not be displayed properly.

Keeping these rules in mind, let us create a basic table for our **Submitted Story** section, where we will put the story titles, authors' names, and submission dates in a table format. Here is the code to do that:

```
{|
| #
| Story Title
| Author
| Submission Date
|-
| 1.
| The Ghost of the Old Mathematician
| J. David
| 12/09/2006
|-
| 2.
| The little Mummy
| W. Patricia
| 13/09/2006
```

```
| -
| 3.
| The Guest
| S. Steve
| 13/09/2006
| -
| 4.
| A true story
| W. Henry
| 15/09/2006
| -
| 5.
| Nightmare
| M. Rahman
| 17/09/2006
| }
```

Now save the page and view it in the browser. We will see something similar to the following:

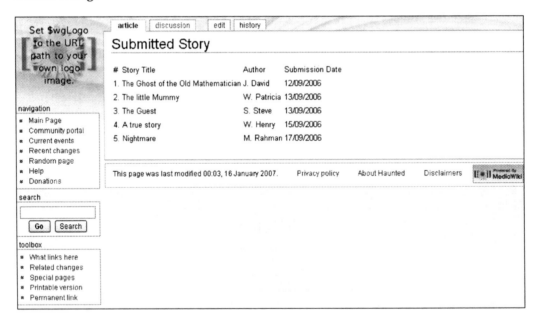

That looks pretty ordinary, doesn't it? The reason is that we made a very basic table. However, there are lots of things that we can do with tables. Here is the list of actions we can perform with wiki tables.

Adding a Caption

MediaWiki provides us with an optional feature of adding a caption to a table. To add a caption to a table, we need to use the table caption syntax (a line followed by a plus sign |+) in the line after the table opening sign.

Adding Column and Row Headers

In order to add a row heading, we have to use the sign ! instead of |. The column heading is also done using the ! sign twice (!!) instead of |. The difference between row and column headings is that the rendering of a row heading depends on the browser-rendering option and the style defined by the author, while a column heading is always rendered bold font by the browser in order to separate it from the column contents.

Let's modify the table in the **Submitted Story** section with what we have learned so far:

```
{|
|+ Story Listing
!# !! Story Title !! Author!! Submission Date
|-
! 1.
| The Ghost of the Old Mathematician
| J. David
| 12/09/2006
|-
! 2.
| The little Mummy
| W. Patricia
| 13/09/2006
|-
! 3.
| The Guest
| S. Steve
| 13/09/2006
|-
! 4.
| A true story
| W. Henry
| 15/09/2006
|-
! 5.
| Nightmare
| M. Rahman
| 17/09/2006
|}
```

`|+ Story Listing` represents the table caption, while `!# !! Story Title !! Author!! Submission Date` represents the table column heading.

Now save the page and view the page in the browser. You will see something similar to this:

Well, it looks a little better than the previous one. Is there anything else we can do to the table? Yes there is. We can define parameters for the table and cells. That means there is a lot of scope for formatting cell and table properties.

Adding Parameters

Wiki syntax supports most of the HTML parameters that are also known as attributes. However, the most important attribute it supports is the style attribute, which we will be using extensively while formatting our tables and cells. The non-supported attributes and tags are very few in number. We have already seen the supported HTML tags in Chapter 3. A few things that should be kept in mind while dealing with parameters are:

- To add parameters to a table, we can use the `style` parameter to define properties related to the table.

- To add parameters to a cell, we can add a parameter list after the line symbol | and close the parameter list using another line symbol | and then put the value of the cell after that. The syntax will look like:
  | Parameter | value.

- We can directly put HTML tags such as `<font>`, `<I>`, etc., inside the cell.

Note: When we add parameters to a table we must keep a space between the parameter list and the table opening syntax.

So what parameters we can define? Definitely we can define many parameters such as color, width, height, border, cells pacing, cell padding, font color, font size, alignment, etc.

The following example contains parameters uses such as border, height, width, background color, and font color:

```
{| style="background:#cccc99;color:black;width:80%;" border="1"
cellpadding="5" cellspacing="0" align="center"
|+ Story Listing
!# !! Story Title !! Author !! Submission Date
|- style="background:white; color:black"
! 1.
| style="width:300px" |The Ghost of the Old Mathematician
| J. David
| 12/09/2006
|- style="background:#f0f0f0; color:black"
! 2.
| The little Mummy
| W. Patricia
| 13/09/2006
|- style="background:white; color:black"
! 3.
| The Guest
| S. Steve
| 13/09/2006
|- style="background:#f0f0f0; color:black"
! 4.
| A true story
| W. Henry
| 15/09/2006
|- style="background:white; color:black"
! 5.
| Nightmare
| M. Rahman
| 17/09/2006
|}
```

In the first line of the example, we have applied the `style` parameter, inside which we have defined background color and foreground color, along with the height and width of the table. After that we have defined a border for the table, cell padding and spacing for each cell, and center alignment for the table. If we move down to line 4 in the example, we will see that we have defined row properties to override the table properties defined at the first line. This is to differentiate the two adjacent rows that we can see in the image. In line 6 we have defined cell properties to make the title cell a little bit wider than other cells.

Let us write down the code in our edit panel and save to see what we actually doing over here. The output for the above input will be similar to this one:

So it is a very good example to look at for major style attributes that we can apply in wiki syntax.

For defining colors with names, MediaWiki supports 16 web colors defined by the HTML 4.01 specification. The list of colors is given in the following table:

Color	HTML 4.01 specification	Color	HTML 4.01 specification	Color	HTML 4.01 specification	Color	HTML 4.01 specification
Black	#000000	Silver	#C0C0C0	Maroon	#800000	Red	#FF0000
Navy	#000080	Blue	#0000FF	Purple	#800080	Fuchsia	#FF00FF
Green	#008000	Lime	#00FF00	Olive	#808000	Yellow	#FFFF00
Teal	#008080	Aqua	#00FFFF	Gray	#808080	White	#FFFFFF

Now we will look at a more challenging example, that of a nested table. We will also include row and column span in our example.

Nested Tables

Nested tables are very important for designing a well-structured interface and organizing our contents. Creating nested tables is simpler as in HTML, if you have a proper view what you are trying to do. We will look at the wiki syntax (**pipe syntax**) to create nested tables and other useful parameters that we can utilize in our design.

As the name implies, a nested table is a table inside another table. The nested table resides in another table's cell. In wiki syntax it is not different. So let's modify our table to incorporate sub-sections under each story title. So after each **Story Title** row, we will add a new table to describe the subsections of the story. So here we go.

For better understanding of the example, we will divide the example into three different parts. The first part will describe nested table creation, the second part will explain column span using the `colspan` attribute, and the last part will focus on `rowspan` attributes. We will explain each code block of the following example:

```
{| style="background:#cccc99;color:black;width:100%;" border="0"
cellpadding="5" cellspacing="2" align="center"
|-
| style="width:50%;background:#f5fffa; border:1px solid #cef2e0;
color:black;align:center;vertical-align:top" |
{| style="color:black;width:99%;background-color:#cef2e0;
font-weight:bold;border:1px solid #a3bfb1;" border="0"
cellpadding="5" cellspacing="2" align="center"
|-
| '''Today's Featured Topic'''
|}
;Residual
:Residual Haunting is the playback of an event in time that is left at
a location. Many haunting scenes are thought to be residual in nature
(footsteps in hallways, seeing someone walking down a certain
staircase, etc.). They are endless loops of the same scene being
played over and over, and they are usually always experienced in the
same location.

;Anniversary
:Anniversary ghosts do, as the title suggests, only appear on an
anniversary of some significance like deaths, birthdays and other
times that held some meaning for the deceased or are of historical
```

significance to them. Since this type of ghost only appears on the anniversary of a special event, it seems likely this type of haunting could be a residual haunting, reenacting a certain event in time on that one day or night.

```
| style="width:50%;background:#f5faff; border:1px solid #cedff2;
color:black;align:center;vertical-align:top" |
{| style="color:black;width:99%;background-color:#cedff2;
font-weight:bold;border:1px solid #a3b0bf;" border="0"
cellpadding="5" cellspacing="2" align="center"
|-
| '''Ghost News Around the World'''
|}
```

* UK Ghost Hunters monthly meeting held on Tuesday, 12th September,2006
* New Ghost sighted at a village in China
* New story book from famous Ghost writer ''Mr. Ghost'' has been published.
* Florida Ghost hunter group arranged a weekly gathering this week for the upcoming haunting tour.
* Ghost hunters community in USA reaches 10,000 members
* Haunted Community in Australia starts the journey.
* Haunted video released by New Jersey Ghost Hunters Community

```
|-
| colspan=2 align=center style="width:50%;background:#faf5ff;
border:1px solid #afa3bf;color:black;align:center;vertical-align:top"
|
{| style="color:black;width:99%;background-color:#ddcef2;
font-weight:bold;border:1px solid #afa3bf;" border="0"
cellpadding="5" cellspacing="2" align="center"
|-
| '''Ghost Picture of the Day'''
|}
```

```
{| style="color:black;width:99%;background-color:#faf5ff;;
border:0px solid #afa3bf;" border="0" cellpadding="5" cellspacing="2"
align="left"
|-
| rowspan=2 | Ghost Picture will be here
| Submitted By: '''Mr. Ghost''' , On: 12/09/2006
|-
| '''Previous Images'''
|}
```

```
|}
```

When we save the example and view it in the browser, we will see the following image:

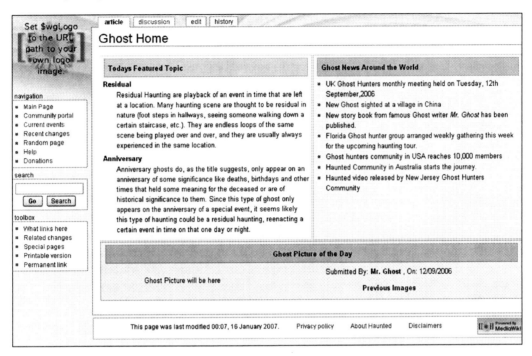

So here is the output for our written code. First we have created a table with two columns. The left column is showing **Today's Featured Topic** and the right is showing **Ghost News Around the World**. In both left and right columns, we have added a boxed title to emphasize the content. We have used nested tables in order to achieve it. Each column now contains another table, which we are referring to as nested tables.

The nested table for **Today's Featured Topic** is created using the following code:

```
{| style="color:black;width:99%;background-color:#cef2e0;
font-weight:bold;border:1px solid #a3bfb1;" border="0"
cellpadding="5" cellspacing="2" align="center"
|-
| '''Today's Featured Topic'''
|}
```

The same goes for the right column nested table. After creating the nested tables for the two columns, we are now looking for a merged column to show the **Ghost Picture of the Day** section. In order to do so, we have used the colspan attribute to merge the columns. After merging the columns, we have created another nested table inside the merged columns in order to create the title box for the picture of the day. Here is the code that performs the cell merging and creation of the nested table for the picture of the day section:

```
|-
| colspan=2 align=center style="width:50%;background:#faf5ff;
border:1px solid #afa3bf;color:black;align:center;vertical-align:top"
|
{| style="color:black;width:99%;background-color:#ddcef2;
font-weight:bold;border:1px solid #afa3bf;" border="0"
cellpadding="5" cellspacing="2" align="center"
|-
| '''Ghost Picture of the Day'''
|}
```

After creating the title table, we have then added one more table. In this table we will show the picture of the day. On the right side of the picture there will be two rows; the first row will show the current picture information while the second one will show the images from the last five days. In order to perform this task, we have used the rowspan attribute of the table, since one of our columns will contain a single row whereas the other one will contain two rows. Here is the code used to create that:

```
{| style="color:black;width:99%;background-color:#faf5ff;;
border:0px solid #afa3bf;" border="0" cellpadding="5" cellspacing="2"
align="left"
|-
| rowspan=2 | Ghost Picture will be here
| Submitted By: '''Mr. Ghost''' , On: 12/09/2006
|-
| '''Previous Images'''
|}
```

So all in all, it's a comprehensive example of wiki table creation using wiki syntax only. You might be wondering, why we have created the section to show the picture of the day but we have not added any image to the table. Wait for a few minutes. We are going to learn about images in a while.

However, we can also create tables using two other approaches. They are:

- **XHTML**: This is a markup language that is a cleaner and stricter version of HTML.

- **HTML and Wiki -td**: This is the HTML way of creating tables in MediaWiki. This is not as strict as XHTML. As a result we can enjoy some flexibilities while creating tables such as not closing the tags. It is not recommended to use this method for creating tables since in future browsers might not support the method.

> Note: The `thead`, `tbody`, `tfoot`, `colgroup`, and `col` elements are currently not supported in MediaWiki.

Out of the three ways for creating tables—XHTML, HTML and Wiki-td, and wiki-pipe—wiki-pipe seems to be the easiest and most convenient to apply, especially for those who do not have HTML table knowledge. The other two options are also very good if you know about HTML tables. However, each of the three options to create tables in MediaWiki has some pros and cons. The following table lists a few differences between them:

Create	XHTML	HTML & Wiki-td	Wiki-pipe
Table	`<table></table>`	`<table></table>`	`{| param` `|}`
Caption	`<caption></caption>`	`<caption></caption>`	`|+ caption`
Row	`<tr></tr>`	`<tr>`	`|-`
Column/data cell	`<td></td>`	`<td>`	`|`
Header	`<th></th>`	`<th>`	`!`

Here are the pros of the three available methods:

XHTML	HTML & Wiki-td	Wiki-pipe
Can be reviewed/debugged with any XHTML editor	Can be previewed/debugged with any HTML editor.	Easy to read
Well-known to the user and developer	Well-known to the user and developer	Easy to write
Easy to read and can be formatted for easier reading	Can be formatted for easier reading	Easy to learn
Well structured, so less chances of user errors	Takes less space than XHTML since tags do not have such strict rules as XHTML	Takes very much less space than the other two

The cons of the three available methods are:

XHTML	HTML & Wiki-td	Wiki-pipe
Sometimes it gets tedious when file gets bigger.	It is not a recommended way to do HTML editing.	Unfamiliar syntax.
		Rigid structure.
		You cannot indent the table for better reading.
Not very easy to read quickly to know what the content is since there are lots of tags.	In the near future it might not be supported by browsers. So it should be avoided.	The signs might be confusing for some people who are familiar with HTML syntax.
Takes a lot of space for the tags.	Confusing, especially for people with little HTML experience since lots of tags don't have closing tags where the rule says there will be a closing tag.	It's nothing but a short cut to the HTML syntax.

File Uploading

In order to make an image link or media file link, the file must be uploaded on the Internet. So, for internal linking the file must be uploaded to the server, and for external linking it must reside in any Internet site. Before continuing with the uploading feature, let me tell you something that we have not come across so far. We will now be accessing the privileged services in MediaWiki, which will require us to be logged in.

Why and How to Log In

Login is necessary for security reasons and user identification. Because we are trying to upload files to the server, logging in will help to keep a track of the users who have uploaded files.

On the screen at the top-right corner we see a link called **Log in / create account**. If we follow the link it will take us to the following page:

If you already have a user name and password for this site, then you can enter the **Username** and **Password,** and click the **Log in** button to get access to the priviledged services. Since so far in this book we have not talked about login, let us assume that we don't have any login account created. So, first we will create an account for a new user named **ghosthunter**. In order to do so, we have to click the **Create an account** link in the **Log in** form. We will be taken to the new user registration page as shown in the following screenshot:

Let's enter all the required information in the fields specified and click the **Create account** button. The account will be created and we will be automatically logged into the system.

Accessing the File Upload Option

Now let's focus on file uploading. In the **Ghost Home** page we have created the picture of the day section to show the best picture of the day. In order to do so, we have to perform the following tasks:

- Upload the image file giving it a unique name.
- Refer to the uploaded file from any page we want in order to create a link.

For file uploading, we need to click on a link named **Upload file** in the **toolbox** section. It does not matter which page you are visiting, you will have the **toolbox** section visible at the left side of the navigation panel. If the link is missing, it is because the uploading system is not enabled by the site administrator. We can confirm whether the **Upload file** option is enabled or not by visiting the **Special pages** section from the **toolbox**. In the **Special pages** list, we have various links, one being **Upload file**, which is at the bottom of the list. If we click the link we will be forwarded to the **Upload file** page. We will see the following page:

Since file uploading is disabled, let's enable the option in our site. Although we haven't gone to the administration section yet, we can still share the knowledge here.

In order to enable the uploading service, perform the following tasks:

1. Open the `Localsettings.php` file from the MediaWiki installation folder.

2. When you open the file you will find a line like that below. If the line is not in the file then add the line to the file.

   `$wgEnableUploads = false;`

3. Change the line to `$wgEnableUploads = true;` in order to enable the file upload. Save the page and refresh the page in your browser.

Now we will see a link in the toolbox section named **Upload file**.

Clicking the link will take us to the **Upload file** screen, which will look like the following image:

Before uploading, you have to make sure that you have the proper permission to upload files and the right file type to upload. The system administrator can block your account from uploading any file if any abuse has been reported against you. We will learn more about the allowed file types and blocked file types in the administration section later in this book. Clicking the **Browse** button will bring a file browsing dialog based on the operating system. Choose your desired file from the dialog.

> The preferred supported types of files in MediaWiki are JPEG for photographic images, PNG for drawings and other iconic images, and OGG for sounds. You can upload other files if the system admin has provided those file extensions in the configuration file. We will learn more about this is in administration chapter later in the book.

There is a text box for **Destination filename** in the **Upload file** page. This option is used for removing ambiguity among users. As it is the very basis of a wiki site that other users will edit your contents, other users might need to upload a file with same name. So a destination file gives user the option to give a filename according to their desire. But what if more than one user gives same **Destination filename**? If this is the case then the first file will be replaced by the later one, but a warning will be given to you as in the following screen:

But don't worry too much about this, since file history keeps track of all the files. You can view your replaced files anytime and revert to the old ones if you want. But in order to avoid such situation, we can perform the following steps:

- Open special pages, go to **File list** page, and perform a search to see if the file name is already taken or not. If it is taken then come up with another suitable name.

- An alternative approach is to put your username followed by the original file name. That will distinguish each file based on user. Since each username is unique, there is no chance of overriding any file name by someone else accidentally. You can still override your own file if required.

1. After giving the proper name in the **Destination filename** box, click the **Upload** button to upload the file. You can also provide a summary for the file if you want. So now let's upload an image file to the server. Why not upload our picture of the day?

2. Choose the file from the local machine using the **Browse** button.

3. We will now rename the destination file to be ghosthunter followed by the file name.

4. Provide a summary for the upload in the **Summary** box.

5. Check the **Watch this page** option if you want to monitor the file and the changes that might occur in future. We will talk more about this option in the chapter about organizing content later in this book.

6. Check the **Ignore any warnings** option if you want to upload the file regardless of any warning. You can bypass any warning by checking this option. It will upload the file irrespective of any warning.

7. Click the **Upload file** button to upload the image.

When uploading is done, the image will appear in the window. It will show the file description and file history at the bottom of the page along with some other links to modify the file. This page is called the image page. We will learn more about image pages in the next section.

What to Upload and What Not

If you want to upload files with other than the preferred file extensions, then it must be allowed by the system administrator in the settings file. The system administrator can allow or disallow any file extension to be used for a file upload. But wait, MediaWiki itself has some file extensions in its black list, which means you cannot upload files with those extensions. The complete list can be found at the MediaWiki installation directory under the `Includes` folder. The `DefaultSettings.php` file contains all the black-listed file extensions. Here is a list of black-listed files and the reasons they are not permitted in general:

File Types	Risk
html, htm, js, jsb	May contain cookie-stealing JavaScript and web bugs
'php', 'phtml', 'php3', 'php4', 'phps'	May Execute Arbitrary Code on the server
shtml', 'jhtml', 'pl', 'py', 'cgi'	May be interpreted by some servers
'exe', 'scr', 'dll', 'msi', 'vbs', 'bat', 'com', 'pif', 'cmd', 'vxd', 'cpl'	May contain harmful executables for Windows victims

Working with Images

An image can be used in the wiki site as internally linked or as externally linked. Internal linking refers to the same project. An image name is assumed to refer to the one in the same project if it exists there. If the image does not exist in the project then the image will not be shown.

An embedded internal image automatically links to the Image page, which shows the full image, or, depending on preferences, a reduced version with a link to the full-size version. The page also provides information about the image.

Image Page

Every uploaded image file is associated with a page where it is shown along with its details. This is known as the Image page. The image description page consists of four parts:

- The image itself
- Description of the image (name, size and type)
- Image history showing the image uploading history
- A list of pages that link to the image

The corresponding image page of our uploaded logo is shown in the following screenshot:

Adding an Image as a Thumbnail

To add the uploaded image to an article as a thumbnail, we can use the following syntax:

```
[[Image: image name including extension |thumb|caption]]
```

Or:

```
[[Image: image name including extension |thumb|width in
pixels|caption]]
```

Or:

```
[[Image: image name including extension |width in pixels|caption]]
```

If we want to create a page where we will use the thumbnail version of the file we have uploaded, then we have to write the following syntax inside the page:

```
[[Image:GhosthunterHaunted.jpg|thumb|100px|Haunted]]
```

Let's add this line to the picture-of-the-day section in our **Ghost Home** page. In the code, replace the line Ghost picture will be here with the above line. This will produce the following page:

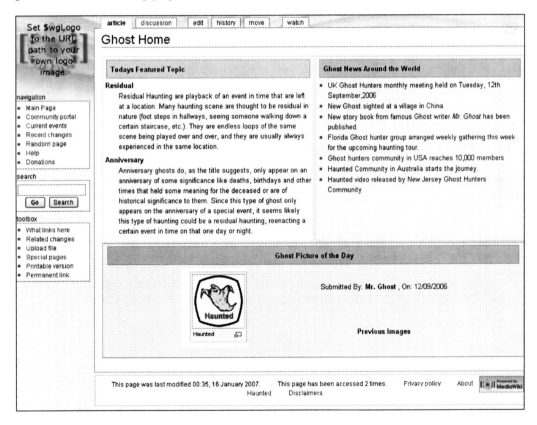

So a thumbnail is automatically created for the big image. When the thumbnail image is clicked it will take us to the corresponding image page. We can also position the image as we want. After the image name line (`Image:...`), put the alignment (right, left, center) and then the remaining syntax and it will show the image in desired position. If you do not specify the alignment for the thumbnail, then the alignment will default to the left. We can also use the caption field as a link. The following link will link to `www.google.com` and show the image in the center:

```
[[Image:GhosthunterHaunted.jpg|center|thumb|100px|Haunted http://www.
google.com]]
```

From MediaWiki 1.5 onwards the default thumbnail width can be set in the preferences, which we will learn about later in this book. So typically it is better *not* to specify the width of the thumbnail, in order to respect the users' preferences unless, for a special reason, a specific size is required regardless of preferences, or a size is specified outside the range of widths (120px-300px) that can be set in the preferences.

For defining an internal wiki link in the caption, we can use the following syntax:

```
[[Image:GhosthunterHaunted.jpg|center|thumb|100px|Haunted [[Story]] ]]
```

Note: If you want to use the image on its own line so that no text is shown on the same line as the image, then use the HTML tag `<br clear="all" />` after the image syntax. If you want to use the frame property where the image will be shown in actual size within a frame, then you can use the frame properties of `image`. The syntax will be like this:

```
[[image:GhosthunterHaunted.jpg| frame |25px| The
little ghost]]
```

To create an inline image we can use the following syntax in our previous image section of the **Ghost Home** page:

```
Yesterday [[image:GhosthunterHaunted.jpg|25px| Saturday Ghost]]   Day
before yesterday[[image:GhosthunterHaunted.jpg|25px| Friday Ghost]]
```

It will produce the following output:

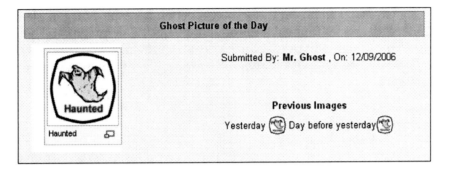

One thing we have to note is that, the text after the last two pipes (Friday Ghost and Saturday Ghost) is not a caption as we have known so far. Instead it is called a title. The basic difference between caption and title is that a caption shows just below the image while a title shows as alternative text when the mouse cursor is taken over the image. It is similar to the `alt` attribute in HTML.

Embedding External Images

External images are not always supported for embedding. Currently they are not supported in many wiki sites and also in MediaWiki by default. However, you can add the following line to the `LocalSettings.php` file or enable the line to allow external images:

```
$wgAllowExternalImages = true;
```

We have already seen this feature in the last chapter. Here is the code snippet from last chapter:

```
For Wiki books: [http://www.packtpub.com/images/PacktLogoSmall.png]
```

This will load the image to the page but in its actual size. It is recommended that if you need to use any image then you download from the other site if copyright is not violated and upload it to your wiki for use. Then we can resize the image and use it according to our needs. But it is always recommended *not* to hotlink for vandalism and bandwidth theft.

Creating a link to an image without creating a thumbnail

If you don't want to display the image, you can link to the file's description page, by adding a colon in the beginning: `[[:GhosthunterHaunted.jpg]]`.

Creating a Gallery in MediaWiki

The last thing we will learn about in the image section is a built-in tag in MediaWiki named "gallery". It creates four columns of thumbnails for an image list. The images must be declared without square brackets inside the `gallery` tag. We can also set captions for the images. In order to create a gallery we have to use the following syntax:

```
<gallery>
Image:{filename}|{caption}
Image:{filename}|{caption}
{...}
</gallery>
```

One good thing about `caption` is that we can provide a wiki link as well as an image link with `caption`. A wiki link or image link without the image name is not allowed, and won't be shown in the gallery. If we place text it inside the gallery tag, it will be shown in the place of the image. If a text entry contains a link, then the whole entry is ignored. Let's look at an example:

```
<gallery>
Image:ghostmap.jpg
Image:Ghost map small.jpg|[[Nevada_map | Nevada Ghost Map]]
Image:UK ghost map.gif | UK ghost Sighted
Image:Phoenix6.gif
Image:Town2.gif
Image:Town4.gif
Image:Town2.gif
Image:Victoria7.gif
Image:Phoenix6.gif
Image:Town2.gif
Image:Victoria7.gif | Search More with [http://www.google.com http://
www.google.com.bd/images/logo_sm.gif]
END
</gallery>
```

And the output is shown in the following image:

Superimposing and Putting Text in Images

Have you ever thought of putting an image on top of another image or adding text to the image without using any image editor? Yes, it is possible simply using a few tags in MediaWiki. This is basically achieved by combining HTML tags and wiki syntax. Since it requires some familiarity with HTML tags, most people might not use this feature. However, these examples are for those who are interested to discover yet another powerful but simple technique of MediaWiki. Before we start, it will be good to tell you something about these techniques. These techniques require some knowledge about positioning of your contents over an existing image. So we have to know the exact location at which to put the contents, or else you will end up with a trial and error method.

An Old Map

Ghost writer, a great contributor for the haunted site, found an old image from a local library. It is a map for ghost locations on the Keweenaw Peninsula in Michigan, USA. In the mid 1800s there were copper fields around the region that were abandoned during the 1920s. Most of the houses there are also haunted. Ghost writer found the following map and wanted to share it with other haunted members.

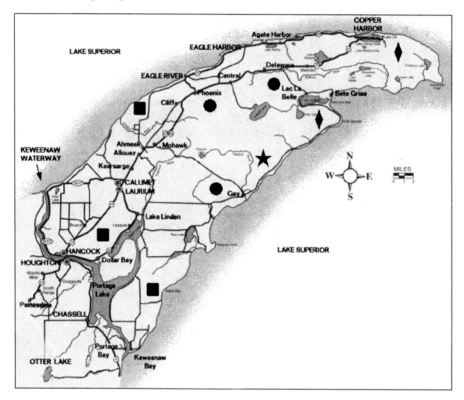

There were a few symbols in the image that are definitely indicating something. Ghost writer was curious to know the significance of the symbols, but there was no legend provided with the image in order to indicate the meaning of those symbols. He went through different books and historical journals, and found the meanings of those symbols. He wants to add a legend to the image at the right bottom corner without altering the image itself. He recreated the symbols and placed them on the original image without destroying the map. First he uploaded the map file (ghostmap.jpg) to the wiki site and then uploaded the symbols for square (square. gif), circle (circle.gif), diamond (diamond.gif), and star (star.gif). Ghost writer already knows the image dimensions for the ghost map and symbols. Since the legends will be shown at the right-bottom corner, he calculated the positions of the legends and wrote the following code:

```
<div style="position: relative">[[Image:ghostmap.jpg]]
<div style="position: absolute; left: 375px; top: 260px"><b>Legend</
b></div>
<div style="position: absolute; left: 375px; top: 280px">[[image:
square.gif]] Ghost House</div>
<div style="position: absolute; left: 375px; top: 300px">[[image:
circle.gif]] Copper Mines</div>
<div style="position: absolute; left: 375px; top: 320px">[[image:
diamond.gif]] Ghost Town</div>
<div style="position: absolute; left: 375px; top: 350px">[[image:star.
gif]] First Ghost Sighted</div>
</div>
```

After he saved the page it looked like this:

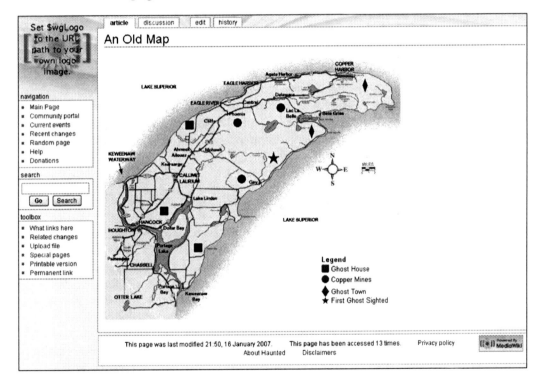

As you can see, the legends are inside the image, and this has been done without altering the image itself. This is known as the "superimposing technique". We have added both images and texts on top of the original image. We have used <div> tags in order to accomplish the task. If you are good at using the <div> tag then you can create various layers of images on top of each other.

One thing about the previous example is that, since we are using inline images, we cannot put links to the legend items via the legend icons. But we can put links for each of the legend descriptions in order to take the readers to details of those places. In order to do so, we have to convert legend descriptions to wiki links. Here is the modified code for the next example:

```
<div style="position: relative">[[Image:ghostmap.jpg]]
<div style="position: absolute; left: 375px; top: 260px"><b>Legend</
b></div>
<div style="position: absolute; left: 375px; top: 280px">[[image:
square.gif]] [[GhosthouseOldmap | Ghost House]]</div>
<div style="position: absolute; left: 375px; top: 300px">[[image:
circle.gif]] [[copperminesOldmap | Copper Mines]]</div>
<div style="position: absolute; left: 375px; top: 320px">[[image:
diamond.gif]] [[ghosttownOldmap | Ghost Town]]</div>
<div style="position: absolute; left: 375px; top: 350px">[[image:star.
gif]] [[ghostsightedOldmap | First Ghost Sighted]]</div>
</div>
```

This will create links from the legend descriptors to the targeted pages (we are assuming that those pages exist). As we can see, we can create superimposed images and texts on any images with the help of HTML tags and Cascading Style Sheet (CSS) properties. Though this is an advanced technique, it is something good to know.

Using Audio with MediaWiki

Other than images, MediaWiki also supports audio and video, but in a very limited manner. The supported audio and video format is Ogg. The version of audio preffered by MediaWiki is **Ogg Vorbis**. Ogg Vorbis is an open and free audio compression codec project from the Xiph.org Foundation. It is frequently used in conjunction with the Ogg container and is then called Ogg Vorbis. The reason MediaWiki chose this format is simply because it's free and best fits with the general aim of allowing access to all, by preventing lock-in from proprietary standards like MP3. Unfortunately, the Ogg format is not well supported by existing sound software, making it important that we inform our users that they might need to install specialized software to create and play these files. Most people are accustomed to, and probably already have, facilities for MP3 playback and recording, but have never heard of Ogg Vorbis. In order to solve these issues, MediaWiki is planning to develop a mechanism to operate Ogg files from the software itself. Since it is still in the development stage, it won't be a good idea to plan to support audio in your wiki site.

Since MediaWiki supports Ogg format, we can upload Ogg files as Media files in our wiki site and make links to others in order to download from the site. An Ogg extension is not added to the default settings property. In order to add support for the Ogg format, we have to add the following line in our `LocalSettings.php` file or modify it to include `'ogg'`, if it is already there:

```
$wgFileExtensions = array( 'png', 'gif', 'jpg', 'jpeg', 'ogg')
```

Using Mathematical Formulas

MediaWiki gives us the opportunity to use mathematical formulas in articles. MediaWiki uses a subset of **TeX markup**, including some extensions from LaTeX and AMSLaTeX, for mathematical formulae. The formulae are shown in a graphical format, such as PNG, or in plain HTML.

In order to create mathematical markup we have to use the `<math>` tag and all the formula syntax will be inside the tag. Extra spaces and line gaps will be ignored inside the tag.

Note: the `<math>` tag does not work by default in the MediaWiki installation. In order to make it work, you have enabled the TeX option from the `LocalSettings.php` file. You have to set `$wgUseTeX` to true (`$wgUseTeX = true;`). Also you have to make sure that Tex is installed on the wiki server and a proper path is defined in the `LocalSettings.php` file..

The rendered PNG images are in black fonts with white background. But the images are not transparent. We can also use HTML special characters for few of the mathematical functionalities:

TeX Syntax	TeX Rendering	HTML Syntax	HTML Rendering
`<math>\alpha\,</math>`	α	`&alpha;`	α
`<math>\sqrt{2}</math>`	$\sqrt{2}$	`&radic;2`	√2
`<math>\sqrt{1-e^2}</math>`	$\sqrt{1-e^2}$	`&radic;(1&minus;''e''&sup2;)`	√(1–e²)

So we can use HTML when required, though HTML does not have all the symbols. But it is advisable to use HTML for available symbols so as to avoid the requirement for a PNG image.

Here is the list of functions and markups that you can use in MediaWiki:

Feature	Syntax	Rendered Output
Standard functions	`\lim n \ \limsup o \ \ liminf p`	$\lim n \ \limsup o \ \liminf p$
Modular arithmetic	`a \bmod b`	$a \bmod b$
Derivatives	`\nabla \; \partial x \; dx \; \dot x \; \ddot y`	$\nabla \ \partial x \ dx \ \dot x \ \ddot y$
Root	`\sqrt [n] {x}`	$\sqrt[n]{x}$
Geometric	`\Diamond \; \Box \; \ triangle \; \angle \; \ perp` `\; \mid \; \nmid \; | \; 45^\circ`	$\Diamond \ \Box \ \triangle \ \angle \ \perp \mid \nmid \ \| \ 45°$
Superscript	`a^2`	a^2
Subscript	`a_2`	a_2
Sum	`\sum_{k=1}^N k^2`	$\sum_{k=1}^N k^2$
Product	`\prod_{i=1}^N x_i`	$\prod_{i=1}^N x_i$
Coproduct	`\coprod_{i=1}^N x_i`	$\coprod_{i=1}^N x_i$
Limit	`\lim_{n \to \infty}x_n`	$\lim_{n \to \infty} x_n$
Integral	`\int_{-N}^{N} e^x\, dx`	$\int_{-N}^{N} e^x \, dx$
Double integral	`\iint_{D}^{W} \, dx\,dy`	$\iint_{D}^{W} dx \, dy$
Quadruple integral	`\iiiint_{F}^{U} \, dx\ ,dy\,dz\,dt`	$\iiiint_{F}^{U} dx \, dy \, dz \, dt$
Intersections	`\bigcap_1^{n} p`	$\bigcap_1^{n} p$
Unions	`\bigcup_1^{k} p`	$\bigcup_1^{k} p$

Feature	Syntax	Rendered Output
Matrices	`\begin{bmatrix} 0 & \` `cdots & 0 \\ \vdots &` `\ddots & \vdots \\ 0 &` `\cdots &` `0\end{bmatrix}`	$\begin{bmatrix} 0 & \cdots & 0 \\ \vdots & \ddots & \vdots \\ 0 & \cdots & 0 \end{bmatrix}$
Case distinctions	`f(n) = \begin{cases}` `n/2, & \mbox{if }n\mbox{` `is even} \\ 3n+1, & \` `mbox{if }n\mbox{ is odd}` `\end{cases}`	$f(n) = \begin{cases} n/2, & \text{if } n \text{ is even} \\ 3n+1, & \text{if } n \text{ is odd} \end{cases}$

These are a very few of the functions that we can use with MediaWiki. We can also use color in our equation:

```
x_{1,2}=\frac{-b\pm\sqrt{\color{Red}b^2-4ac}}{2a}
```

We can also write complex mathematical equations based on the syntax we have seen so far.

```
<math>f(x) = \begin{cases}1 & -1 \le x < 0 \\
\frac{1}{2} & x = 0 \\ 1 - x^2 & 0 < x\le 1\end{cases}</math>
```

The generated output will be:

$$f(x) = \begin{cases} 1 & -1 \le x < 0 \\ \frac{1}{2} & x = 0 \\ 1 - x^2 & 0 < x \le 1 \end{cases}$$

Magic Words

Magic words are a few reserved words that are used for special purposes in MediaWiki. They are used to create special types of formatting. We can use magic words to show table of contents, display the current date and time, etc. A list of magic words in MediaWiki and their description is provided in the following table:

Magic word	Explanation
__NOTOC__	Hides Table of Content on the current page.
__FORCETOC__	Forces the table of contents to appear.
__TOC__	Places a Table of Content here.
__NOEDITSECTION__	Hides the edit links beside headings.

Magic word	Explanation
__NOCONTENTCONVERT_ ___NOCC__	Don't perform the content language conversion (character and phase) in article display.
__NOTITLECONVERT__ __NOTC__	Like __NOCC__ but affecting article title only.
__END__	Allows for trailing white space to be included in the page save.

There are a few magic words for formatting and time display:

Magic word	Example	Explanation
{{LC:}}	{{LC:WikI}} = wiki	Converts to lowercase.
{{UC:}}	{{UC:WikI}} = WIKI	Converts to uppercase.
{{LCFIRST:}}	{{LCFIRST:Wiki}} = wiki	Lowercase first character.
{{UCFIRST:}}	{{LCFIRST:wiki}} = Wiki	Uppercase first character.
{{CURRENTDAY}}	14	Displays the current day in numeric form.
{{CURRENTDAY2}}	14	Displays the current day in numeric form (and with a leading zero if less than 10).
{{CURRENTDAYNAME}}	Friday	Displays the current day in named form.
{{CURRENTDOW}}	5	Displays the current day as a number of the week (0=Sunday, 1=Monday etc.).
{{CURRENTMONTH}}	04	Displays the current month in numeric form.
{{CURRENTMONTHNAME}}	April	Displays the current month in named form.
{{CURRENTTIME}}	21:45	Displays the current time of day (hours:minutes).
{{CURRENTWEEK}}	15	Displays the number of the current week (1-52).
{{CURRENTYEAR}}	2006	Returns the current year.

There are other types of magic words available in MediaWiki such as image modifiers, pages, locations and URLs, etc., and this list is always growing. By the time the book is printed, there will be many magic words included that you cannot find here. So it will be useful to visit the list of magic words in the MediaWiki site at the following URL:

```
http://meta.wikimedia.org/wiki/Help:Magic_words.
```

Summary

In this chapter we learned about images, tables, lists, and other advanced formatting techniques. We have also seen how easy it is to use wiki syntax to create attractive and sophisticated designs. In the process we have created lot of content. Now it is time for us to organize our content before we loose track of what we have created so far. So let us move on to the next chapter, where we will learn all about organizing and managing our content.

5
Organizing Content

So far we have learned about formatting techniques and content creation procedures. However, it is also important to organize the content that we are creating. Managed content looks much better than haphazard content for both authors and readers. Since MediaWiki works in a multi-user environment, it is necessary to maintain well organized content so that editing and reviewing become easier for users. In this chapter we will see:

- Why organizing content is important for our site
- The available features in MediaWiki for content organization
- How we can move pages in the wiki environment
- Using special pages for making our life easier

Necessity of Organizing Content

As the site grows, the numbers of users and articles also grow. The necessity of organized content arises because:

- As the number of users keeps growing, the articles and other contents such as images, media files, etc., will keep growing. In order to maintain the large number of articles and content, we need a proper structured system to organize all the content. Think of a library where hundreds and thousands of books are kept. If those books are not kept in order, then where should a person look for a particular book? For users, it will be really nice to have proper organized content rather than disjoint and unorganized content.

- As the number of articles keeps growing, it is also necessary to categorize them. It is very easy to find a particular article and maintain it based on the category. Carrying on our library example, if we keep a section for horror books, and under this section we keep relevant comics, stories, novels, and movies, then it will be much easier for someone to point to the horror section and find the right movie there. One thing we have to remember: the more organized a site is, the more user friendly it is. Users love sites that are friendly to use and adopt.

- Sometimes it is required to break an article in several pages as the article is very big and difficult to maintain on a single page. Users usually have to scroll through the huge amount of text, and this can be problematic. Also, editing a huge amount of content at once can be difficult. So we need to know how we can manage such big articles by breaking them into sub-pages and also keeping them together so that user can find them easily.

MediaWiki can help us in this regard. MediaWiki has some built-in features that can make our task very easy and simple. These software features are very important components of MediaWiki since organizing in a collaborative community is not that easy. We will now focus on a few MediaWiki features that can be used for better content organization.

MediaWiki Content Organizing Features

MediaWiki handles these major issues without any problem or complexity whatsoever. The concept and the application of organizing content in MediaWiki are easy to grasp and apply. MediaWiki has the following software features to strengthen its organizing ability.

- Namespaces
- Categories
- Templates
- Sections
- Redirection

We will now explore each of the features in detail with examples.

Namespaces

Namespaces are used to group together similar type of contents. Namespaces divide a wiki into different areas so that each functional area is clearly defined. Namespaces can segregate different types of content that may exist under the same title. Generally, namespaces should not be used to categorize content of the same type—we can use categories for that.

The namespaces that come with MediaWiki illustrate this "content type" distinction:

- The `Main`, un-prefixed, namespace is for the primary content to be maintained in the wiki.
- The `Talk` namespaces are for discussion.
- The `Project` namespace is for policies, votes, and meta-information.
- The `Image` namespace is for images.

Namespaces allow separation of content for better management. One thing about a namespace is that it is not created by the users themselves. MediaWiki has some pre-defined namespaces and administration can add new namespaces if required. The namespaces that are added by the administrator are known as **custom namespaces**. It is always important to let users know about the custom namespaces available in the site.

One surprising fact is that we have already used namespaces in our Haunted site without noticing. How? Well, do you remember the image upload feature that we used in last chapter? It uploaded the image to the `Image` namespace, as all the images are stored in an `Image` namespace. Like the `Image` namespace, there are 17 other namespaces available in MediaWiki for special purposes.

So when should one create a custom namespace? Essentially, if you have some type of content that you feel is substantially different from the content in the existing namespaces, you may want to consider creating a new namespace. For our Haunted site, we can have a `movie` namespace, so as to accommodate movie descriptions and trailers. Now let us focus on how we can use namespaces.

A page title in MediaWiki is consists of two parts separated by a colon (`:`). The part before the colon is the (optional) namespace, and the part after the colon is the required page title. An example page title with a namespace is `Help:Namespace`, which will take us to the Namespace page under the `Help` namespace.

So far, the pages we have created did not have any namespace prefixed to them. Where do those pages belong? Are they without a namespace? No, even they belong to a namespace—the `Main` namespace. A page title without a colon belongs to the `Main` namespace. There are as many as 18 namespaces in MediaWiki, among which two are used as pseudo namespace, and 16 separate namespaces are defined by MediaWiki. Although there are 16 defined namespaces in MediaWiki, eight of them are talk pages of remaining eight namespaces.

> A **talk page** is a special type of page used for discussions. On a talk page, users can communicate as in a forum. They can write their views or share their ideas on certain topics. Every page and namespace has an associated talk page (except for the `Special` namespace). Since talk pages mostly involve multiple users, we will learn more about talk pages in the next chapter, where we will discuss the multi-user environment in MediaWiki.

Here is a list of 18 namespaces in MediaWiki and a summary of their functionalities:

Namespace	Functionality
Media	This is the first pseudo namespace in MediaWiki. It is used for uploaded files.
Special	This is the second and last pseudo namespace in MediaWiki. It is used for listing all special pages.
Main	This is the core namespace that holds all the pages without specifying any namespace in front of the title. Pages under this namespace are also known as normal pages. The content we have added so far to our Haunted site is inside the `Main` namespace.
Talk	The `Talk` namespace holds talk pages for the `Main` namespace. Talk pages are used for discussion. The `Talk` namespace is used for all the discussion pages under the `Main` namespace.
User	This namespace is used for every registered user in MediaWiki. Every registered user has a homepage, and all homepages are stored under the `User` namespace and can be accessed by a `User:username` link. Users can use this page as their profile page.
User_talk	User talk pages are used for discussions on user pages.
Project	This namespace provides information about the current project or wiki, such as guidelines, ideas, future plans, etc.
Project_talk	This talk page is used for the `Project` namespace.
Image	Used for images and other uploaded file information. Description of the file such as file size, version, etc., can be found here.
Image_talk	This is the talk page for the `Image` namespace.
MediaWiki	This namespace is used for system messages defined for the current wiki or project. These messages are either editable by a registered user, or sysops can turn off editing for security reasons.
MediaWiki_talk	This is the talk page for the `MediaWiki` namespace.
Template	This is used as the default namespace for templates, another feature that is used for integrating a page into another page. We will learn about templates later in this chapter.

Namespace	Functionality
Template_talk	This is the talk page for the Template namespace.
Help	This is typically used for building help content for wiki users. All the help-related information is stored here.
Help_talk	This is the talk page for the Help namespace.
Category	Pages can be put into categories. The Category namespace shows a list of categories inside the wiki, and upon clicking a category, a list of pages under the category along with additional text is also shown.
Category_talk	This is the talk page for the Category namespace.

Creating New Pages in a Namespace

Though we have 18 namespaces altogether, we cannot create new pages in all the defined namespaces. Most pages in a namespace are generated automatically by the system itself, and hence new pages cannot be added to them. It is also not recommended to alter anything that is defined by MediaWiki.

Special pages are generated during installation. After that we cannot add any new pages to the Special namespace. Media and image pages are created when a file is uploaded to the server. So we cannot create a new page in these cases unless we upload a file to the server. It's the same with the User namespace, where all active users have their own pages, which are generated during user registration. Talk pages are generated automatically with their respective pages. So we are very much limited as far as accessing namespaces for adding new pages is concerned. We can add content to the Main, Project, Template, Help, and Category namespaces as well as to custom namespaces (if any).

To create a new page or access an already existing page in a namespace, we can recall our knowledge of creating a new page. We simply have to write the page title after the namespace's name followed by a colon in the address bar of the browser. For example, Help:How to use Namespace will create a page inside the Help namespace with the title **How to use Namespace** if the page does not exist. If the page exists, then this will take us to that page.

> If the given *namespace* is not recognized by MediaWiki or does not exist, then the page will be generated inside the Main namespace. In other words, if the *namespace* does not exist, then it will not be created automatically by the system.

One thing we have to remember is that a page can exist in only one namespace at a time. A single page cannot reside in two namespaces. Separate namespaces can contain pages with the same title, but can't contain the same page. Another important thing to remember is that there is no way in which you can view all the available namespaces on a site. Unless explicitly expressed by the site administrator, it is not possible for visitors to know about the available and custom namespaces other than the default ones.

Category

Have you ever visited Wikipedia for your favorite "James Bond" movie? You will find that there is a category on James Bond movies, and it looks like this:

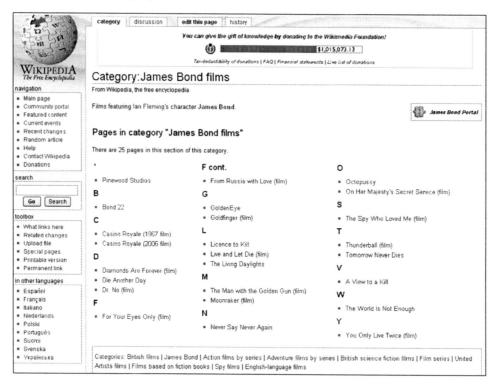

They have actually put all the James Bond movies under a single category so that visitors can find everything under this category. This is a very good and effective way of organizing content, and can be achieved through MediaWiki's "category" feature.

We have seen that namespaces cannot be created by users as they have some limitations. We need a feature that helps us categorize the content that is similar in type and work without any intervention from an administrator or privileged users. MediaWiki has a feature called category, which solves this problem.

Creating a Category

To create a category page, we must add a colon (:) in front of the Category tag. So the tag for creating a category will be:

```
[[:Category:Category name]]
```

The tag has to be typed in the edit box and then the page has to be saved. This will show the category link at the bottom of the page, and a click on this link will take us to the edit page for that category, where we will see an edit box similar to that for a normal wiki page. The key difference between a normal wiki page and a category page is that in a category page the articles and subcategories are displayed in an alphabetical order. These cannot be edited by the users.

The alphabetical order of a category list follows the sequence shown in the following information box. It is based on the **Unicode** order. Here is a partial list of the order sequence that MediaWiki follows:

```
!"#$%&'()*+,-./0123456789:;<=>?@ABCDEFGHIJKLMNOPQ
RSTUVWXYZ[\]^_'abcdefghijklmnopqrstuvwxyz{|}~
```

Note that 1 comes before A, and z comes before a. In the category listing page, the order will be maintained in this manner. For the complete ordering list you can visit the following URL: http://meta.wikimedia.org/wiki/Help:Alphabetic_order.

A category page contains following information:

- Page content or editable text, which can be edited using the **edit** link in the page just like a normal wiki page.

- A list of subcategories, along with the number of subcategories; if there are no subcategories, the header and count are not shown.

- A list of pages in the category, excluding subcategories and images. The number of items in this list is called the number of articles; if there are none, the header is shown anyway, and **there are 0 articles in this category**.

- A list of images with thumbnails (without the number). The first 20 characters of the image name are shown, with an ellipsis if that is not the full name; the file size is also shown.

- A list of parent categories. Categories are separated by the pipe character if there is more than one category for the page.

Putting a Page into a Category

A page in any namespace can be put in a category by adding a category tag to the page. The syntax for this is:

```
[[Category:Category name]]
```

If the category name specified in this tag exists, then the page will be added to the category. However, if the category does not exist, then MediaWiki will first create the category and then add the page information to the category. Categories provide automatic indexes that are useful as tables of contents. The category tag lists the page on the appropriate category page automatically, and also provides a link at the bottom of the page to the category page, which is in the namespace Category. Pages can be included in more than one category by adding multiple category tags. Suppose one of our ghost stories "A night in the jungle" belongs to the short story, real-life story, and self-experience categories. Then to indicate that it belongs to these three categories, we need to add the following tags in the story page:

```
[[Category:short story]]
[[Category:real life story]]
[[Category:self experience]]
```

The categories will then show up at the bottom of the story page, separated by the pipe character as follows:

Categories: Short story | Real life story | Self experience

Category links do not appear at the location where we inserted the tag, but at a fixed place, depending on the skin we have chosen. Category tags may be placed anywhere in the article, although they are typically added to the end of the article to avoid undesirable text-display side effects. Category links are displayed in the order they occur in the article.

Unlike a namespace, a single page can reside in any number of categories that you define. The following example demonstrates the key differences between a namespace and a category.

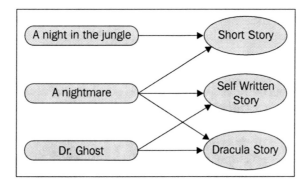

As we can see, a single story can reside in more than one category, which is very efficient in the sense that we don't have to create the page more than once for the categorization. The category just holds the reference of the page; so the overhead of page creation and space is not a consideration here.

Creating Subcategories

Subcategory creation is as simple as category creation, and the good thing about it is that there is no separate syntax for creating a subcategory. We have to use the same tag as we used for creating a category here. However, one thing we have to remember is that since there is not special syntax that will describe category B as a subcategory of category A, we must follow a rule for creating subcategories, which we will call the **bottom up** rule. Look at the following picture:

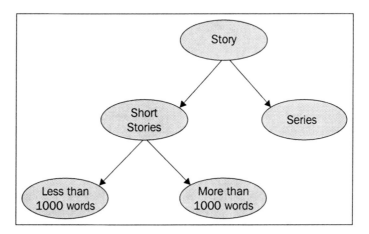

We have divided our story section into two subcategories: **Short Stories** and **Series**. The short stories section is also divided into two subcategories: **Less than 1000 words** and **More than 1000 words**. In order to indicate that Story has subcategories called Short Stories and Series, we have to put the category tag in both the Short Stories and Series pages to indicate that they are subcategories of the Story category. The syntax will be exactly like this in the two pages:

```
[[Category:Story]]
```

The story page now has two subcategories. One good aspect of categories is that they can be nested, i.e. one category can have multiple subcategories and each subcategory can have multiple subcategories, and in this manner the tree can keep going deeper. In the previous example, we have two levels of subcategories. So as we can see, we have to go to the subcategories first to indicate their parent category, and in this way we move from the bottom of the hierarchy to the top. That's why I call this the **bottom up** rule.

Here is an example of a subcategory page:

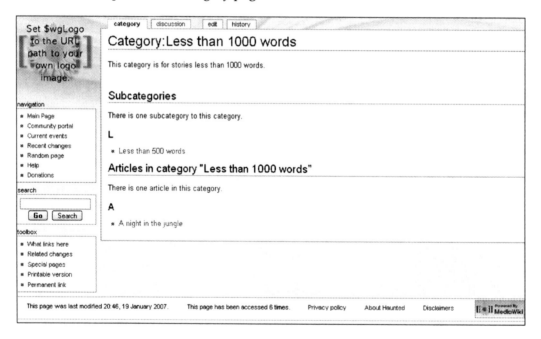

As you can see from the example screenshot, both subcategories and parent categories shown in the page are the just immediate parents or subcategories. For "story", we have the subcategory "short story". For "short story" we have subcategory "less than 1000 words". So when we are in the story page, it shows the subcategory as "short story", and not the "less than 1000 words" subcategory.

How to View the Category List

We have a separate page dedicated to viewing the category list for the wiki site. From the toolbox section on your left navigation panel, click on the **Special pages** link. It will take you to the list of all the special pages under the wiki site. You will see that there is a link named **categories**. Upon clicking the link, you will be redirected to the category page where all the categories and subcategories are listed. You can also add **Special:Categories** to the end of the page URL to come to this page. The category listings are shown alphabetically on the page.

Using Sort Keys to Sort Category Listings

When we are in any category page, we can see listings of subcategories and articles for this category. Most of the time, articles are listed according to their title. So in alphabetic order, the first character of the title influences the order of the article. Sometimes it becomes necessary to put the article in a different order without changing the title. How can we do that? Well, we can do that using a feature called **sort keys** in MediaWiki. Sort keys are used with category specification in an article using the category tag. The sort key, which is also known as the **alternative name**, is written with a pipe character after the category name, as follows:

```
[[Category:category name|sort key]]
```

So suppose we have a page title "**A night in the jungle**". According to the convention, it will be listed under **A** in alphabetic order. However, if we want to list it under **J**, then we have to write the category syntax as:

```
[[Category:real life story|Jungle Night]]
```

or simply as:

```
[[Category:real life story|J]]
```

So when we view the category page, we will see:

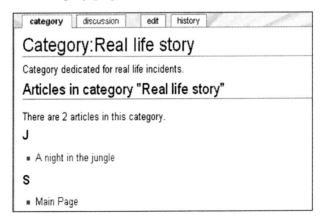

This is a great way of showing and sorting the article listing. However, we have to be careful about the sorting. The sort key is case sensitive; so a page with the tag `[[Category:real life story|Jungle Night]]` will come before a page with the tag `[[Category:real life story|a night in jungle]]`, according to the alphabetic ordering of the listing.

Template

Consider a case where the Haunted site's users felt that they should make a repository of all haunted movies and share it with others. A movie, however, will have a lot of information to go with it—producers, director, actors, release date, distributors, storyline, etc. It will be very easy to create a page with all the information, but it won't be possible to summarize the movie in a way that anybody can have summary information when they visit any movie's page. There needs to be a common format that will be used by all the movie pages. That is how Wikipedia shows a summary of every James Bond movie at the right side of the page. Since all movies have some common attributes but different values, they use the same format for all the James Bond movie summaries—it's only the attributes' values that change, and not the attributes themselves. Can we use the same thing in our Haunted site?

MediaWiki has the solution, and it is known as a template. A **template** is a page that can be inserted into another page via a process called **transclusion**. Templates usually reside in the `Template` namespace in MediaWiki. Templates are useful for any text for which one wants a copy in two or more pages, and there is no need for each copy to be edited independently, to adapt it to the page it is in. Templates can also be parameterized—we can add parameters to a template in order to show different content based on the parameter. This lets a template act like a subroutine. Looking at it from other angle, a template can be thought of as being like the include file that we use in programming.

Creating our First Template

The syntax for insertion of the page `Template:templatename` is `{{ templatename }}`. This is called a template tag. If the page `Template:templatename` does not exist, then `{{ templatename }}` works as `[[Template:templatename]]`, a link to a non-existing page, leading to the edit page for the template. Thus, one way of creating a template is putting in the tag first, and then following the link. Let's create our first template using this technique. Write down the following text in the URL section of the browser:

```
http://haunted.com/index.php?title=Template:Movie_Summary
```

This will take us to an empty non-existent template page. We can edit the template and save it as our template. Let's make the movie summary information template for our movie section. It will contain the movie name, a poster, screenwriter, cast details, etc. Editing a template page is similar to editing a normal page. There is no difference at all, and so we can use wiki syntax in our template page. Let us add the following content in our template page for a movie named **"The Haunting"** and save it:

```
'''The Haunting''' <br>
[[Image:200px-The_Haunting_film.jpg]] <br>
'''The Haunting''' film poster <br>
'''Directed by'''      Jan de Bont<br>
'''Produced by'''      Donna Roth,<br>
Colin Wilson<br>
'''Written by'''       Novel:<br>
Shirley Jackson <br>
'''Screenplay:'''<br>
David Self<br>
'''Starring'''   Lili Taylor,<br>
Catherine Zeta-Jones,<br>
Owen Wilson,<br>
Liam Neeson<br>
'''Distributed by'''    DreamWorks<br>
'''Release date(s)'''   July 20, 1999<br>
'''Running time'''      113 minutes<br>
'''Language'''   English<br>
'''Budget'''       ~ US$80,000,000<br>
```

We can now call this template from any of our pages using a pair of double curly braces {{ }} with the name of the template between the braces. Assuming that we are creating a new page where we will show all stories, let's add the template to a story page. Open any of the story pages that we have created so far, and add the following line at the beginning of the edit page:

```
{{Movie_Summary}}
```

Now save the page and preview it in the browser. You will see true magic now; the content of the template is shown in the story page as follows:

We put the template tag at the start of the page, but you can always put it anywhere you want in the content page. We can use templates to create a header, a footer, the copyright information, special messages, etc., for our site. This is a very simple but powerful use of templates. Think about a situation where we have a lot of movie information available. What we did is just for a single movie, but we can use the same template for other movies with the same type of attributes. When we use templates, we don't have to worry about changing the summary attributes in each and every page. We will just change the template and all the pages will be updated, since pages include that template. We can do amazing things using templates. Also, since they are similar to normal pages, we can always create nice-looking templates using tables, images, links, etc.

Templates work on a project basis. So a template in one wiki will not work in another wiki site. In order to use the same template on another wiki site, we have to build the same template in that site. Also when we change a template, we must be careful about the impact of the changes in the pages where the template is actually used.

Parameterizing Templates

We already know that we can add parameters in our template to make it work like a subroutine. I hope all of you know what a subroutine means; if not you could visit the following URL: `http://en.wikipedia.org/wiki/Subroutine`. Based on its parameters, a subroutine performs some task and shows results. We know templates are not subroutines, but they can be used as subroutines for performing different tasks.

Take the example of our movie summary template. We have hardcoded the name of the movie and other attributes, but we can use the same template for another movie by changing the attributes' values. So it is almost same as adding the content in each page. However, if we can parameterize the template, it will definitely make our task easy.

What we can do is make the movie name, movie poster, writer, actors' names etc., into variables that will be set by parameters and passed from the calling page. All the template parameters are divided into two categories: named parameters and numbered parameters. In order to create a parameterized template, we need to perform the following two tasks every time:

1. In the template page, declare parameters that will be changed based on the passed values.

2. Call the template with proper values from the calling page.

Parameters are declared with three pairs of braces with the parameter name inside. `{{{myVar}}}` declares a parameter name `myVar`. So in the template, the parameter declaration will done as follows:

```
{{{parname1|default}}}, {{{parname2|default}}}
```

and in the tag or calling page, we have to write it as follows:

```
{{templatename|parname1=parvalue1|parname2=parvalue2}}
```

The `default` option in the parameter declaration is totally optional. It can be different for each and every parameter, and applies when no value has been provided for the parameter. Here `default` stands for the default value of the parameter. This default value will be used if a parameter is not set to any value from the calling pages.

You will see that we are using the parameter name in both template definition *and* declaration page. This is known as a **named parameter**. There is another type of parameter as well, called a **numbered parameter**, which is indicated by the use of a number instead of a name. In a numbered parameter option, the declaration looks like this:

```
{{{1|default}}}, {{{2|default}}}
```

and in the calling page, we have to write down the tag as follows:

```
{{templatename|parvalue1|parvalue2}}
```

Now back to our movie summary example. We want to convert our movie summary template to a named parameterized template. We will use different parameters for different attributes of the template. We will also use a table to make the template look better. Here is the code for the template:

```
{|style="width:250px; " border="0"
|-
|width=100px|
|width=100px|
|-
| colspan="2" align="center" |'''{{{name}}}'''
|-
| colspan="2" align="center" |[[Image:{{{image}}}
|{{{image_size|200px}}}]]
|-
| colspan="2" align="center" |''{{{caption}}}''
```

```
|-
|'''Directed by'''||{{{director}}}
|-
|'''Produced by'''||{{{producer}}}
|-
|'''Written by'''||{{{writer}}}
|-
|'''Screenplay:'''||{{{screenplay}}}
|-
|'''Starring'''||{{{starring}}}
|-
|'''Distributed by''' ||{{{distributor}}}
|-
|'''Release date(s)'''||{{{released}}}
|-
|'''Running time'''||   {{{runtime}}}
|-
|'''Language'''||      {{{language}}}
|-
|'''Budget'''||  {{{budget}}}
|}
```

Now save the template and go to the "Haunted Movie" page, where we have included this template. We need to add parameters to the tag, and pass values to the parameters. Write the following tag at the top of the edit box:

```
{{Movie_Summary |
   name      = The Haunting |
   image             = 200px-The_Haunting_film.jpg |
   caption   = ''The Haunting'' film poster |
   writer = '''Novel:'''<br>[[Shirley Jackson]] |
   screenplay = [[David Self]] |
   starring      = [[Lili Taylor]],<BR>[[Catherine
   Zeta-Jones]],<br>[[Owen Wilson]],<br>[[Liam Neeson]] |
   director      = [[Jan de Bont]] |
   producer      = [[Donna Roth]],<br>[[Colin Wilson]] |
   distributor   = [[DreamWorks]] |
   released   = [[July 20]], [[1999]] |
   runtime       = 113 minutes |
   language = English |
   budget        = ~ US$80,000,000
}}
```

After saving the page, you will see that the page looks the same with parameterized values. Here is the page we will be shown on the screen:

Change the values of the parameters, and you will see the difference. We can easily created hundreds and thousands of movie pages with the help of this template. What we need to do is call the template with parameter values, and the template will do the rest.

The same task can be performed with numbered parameters. The numbered parameters will start from 1 and continue until all the parameters are numbered. For numbered parameters, the declaration in the template definition page will be as follows:

```
{|style="width:250px; " border="0"
|-
|width=100px|
|width=100px|
|-
| colspan="2" align="center" |'''{{{1}}}'''
|-
| colspan="2" align="center" |[[Image:{{{2}}}]]
|-
| colspan="2" align="center" |'''{{{3}}}'''
|-
|'''Directed by'''||{{{4}}}
|-
|'''Produced by'''||{{{5}}}
|-
|'''Written by'''||{{{6}}}
|-
|'''Screenplay:'''||{{{7}}}
|-
|'''Starring'''||{{{8}}}
|-
|'''Distributed by'''  ||{{{9}}}
|-
|'''Release date(s)'''||{{{10}}}
|-
|'''Running time'''||  {{{11}}}
|-
|'''Language'''||    {{{12}}}
|-
|'''Budget'''||  {{{13}}}
|}
```

and the calling page tag will look like the following, with changed parameters to create a different movie summary with the same template:

```
{{Movie_Summary
|The Haunting
|200px-The_Haunting_Poster.jpg
|The Haunting DVD cover
|[[Robert Wise]]
|[[Robert Wise]]
|'''Novel:'''<br>[[Shirley Jackson]]
|[[Nelson Gidding]]
```

```
|[[Julie Harris]]<br />[[Richard Johnson]]<br />[[Claire Bloom]]
|[[MGM]]
|[[September 18]], [[1963]] ([[USA]])
|112 min.
|[[English language|English]]
|
}}
```

The output of the page will be:

So we can see that by changing the attributes' values we can use the same template in any page we want. This helps organize the content more effectively and also give a different identity to different types of content.

Named versus Numbered Parameters

Even though both named and numbered parameters can be used, there are some places where named parameters are better than numbered parameters, and vice versa. Here are some things to help you choose between named and numbered parameters.

Named parameters are used when you know which parameters exist, and their exact name. So knowing the name of the parameters is a must for named parameters. Also, we can always mix the order of parameters in the parameter list, and so, no particular order is fixed for a named parameter list. We can make one of our own, until we have all the required parameters in the list. Named parameters are also very easy to understand. We can define a meaning and purpose for the parameter.

For numbered parameters, on the other hand, we don't have to write the parameter's name followed by an assignment operator; we just pass the parameter separated by a pipe character. What is important here, however, is that the order of the parameters *must* be maintained, or else parameters will get wrong values. Numbers are international and they don't need translation for different languages or projects. So unlike named parameters, numbered parameters do not require any translation of the parameter list for using with multilingual sites.

Section

In Chapter 3 we saw how to create sections on a particular page. Sections are an efficient way of organizing content inside a page, since they allow us to generate a table of contents automatically, as well as let us edit section contents rather than page content all at once. Each section in an article has a corresponding **Edit** link on the right side of the section. This link takes us to the article edit page, but with that particular section only. Isn't it amazing? Suppose an article has a 100 sections, and we wanted to edit it. Conventionally, we would have to go through a huge page of 100 sections in the edit box, which will not only look very cumbersome, but will also be very difficult to trace and edit. Sections help us in this matter by ensuring that we get only the relevant section's content while leaving other sections' content untouched, and ensuring that users don't get lost in the huge amount of content. If a page is large, we can also break it into different sub-pages, but that is not always right thing to do. Let's see a comparison between using sections and creating separate pages for a big article.

Comparison between Sections and Separate Pages

Section	Separate pages
Article page contains all the edit histories for the article, not based on section.	Edit histories are stored separately for each page, and can be traced easily.
Article page contains what links here or back links as a whole.	Each page contains the back links, giving more flexibility.
Users can be redirected to a section very easily.	Redirection to a section is not possible.
Loading one large page is more convenient than loading several small ones.	Loading a small page is faster than loading a large page.
Searching within one large page with a local search function is faster, and in some respects better than searching several pages.	Searching separate pages always takes time.
Table of contents is generated providing convenient navigation.	No table of contents is available if we create a separate page for each section.
A single page is always more manageable, since all the contents are in a single place.	Managing many separate pages is difficult, and always needs continuous monitoring for updating.

Creating a Table of Contents Using Sections

In Chapter 3 we learned that sections or headers can be used to create a table of contents for any article. If the article contains more than three sections, then a table of contents is automatically generated. We can also stop the automatic creation of a table of contents by following the methods:

- Turning it off in the user preference settings (we will learn user preference setting in next chapter).
- In the article edit box, making use of the magic word _NOTOC_.

We can also force the system to show a table of contents even when we have less than three sections in the article. This can be performed by adding the _FORCETOC_ or _TOC_ magic words inside the article. If we use the _FORCETOC_ magic word, then the table of contents is placed before the first header in the article, but if we use the _TOC_ magic word in the article, the table of contents is placed at the position of the _TOC_ word in the article. This gives a great flexibility in moving the table of contents to our desired position, such as to the right, center, or left, or inside a table, and in choosing the number of times we want to show the table of contents in the article.

Redirection

As the name suggest, redirection is the process in which users are redirected to a particular page based on the setup or action defined by someone. Most of us have some familiarity with redirection—when we visit a website online, and that site has been moved, we see a little redirection message, and in a few seconds we are moved to a new page. There are a lot of other places where you would find redirection required. When a page in MediaWiki is moved or renamed, a redirection is created automatically by the system.

A redirect is a page with only the following kind of content:

```
#REDIRECT [[link in internal link style]]
```

So far we know that a redirect is used for page movement and renaming in MediaWiki. However, redirects can be used for other purposes too.

- Finding a page.
- Conveniently going to a page.
- Linking indirectly to a page, without the need for a piped link.

In order to create a redirect, we have to create a new page or use an existing page from the site. If the page is new, then add the following line at the beginning of the edit box:

```
#REDIRECT [[A night in the jungle]]
```

Suppose the redirect page we have just created is named "Story". Now, whenever someone tries to access the "Story" page, he or she will be redirected to the "A night in the jungle" page. When the user is redirected to the page, he or she will see a small caption at the top of the page, citing details of the page from which they have been redirected:

Editing a redirect is as simple as creating it. Click the redirect page's name from any of the pages where you see the text **Redirected from** …. This will take you to the redirect page. Edit the page as you would a normal page, and save it.

We can add additional text after the redirect tag and the link. This can be used as an explanation when we visit the redirect page itself. Extra lines of text are automatically deleted when saving the redirect. The page will not redirect if there is anything on the page before the redirect. Also, there must be no spaces between the # and the REDIRECT. We have to also remember that interwiki redirects and special page redirects are not possible with the current features. Also, redirecting to an anchor is not possible.

An Alternative for Namespaces

A project or a wiki can be used instead of creating namespaces. This is sometimes advantageous, but at times is just overkill. Suppose we want to create a multilingual site for our Haunted information. So there will be a German site, an English site, a Spanish site, etc. There are two ways we can do that: we can create separate namespaces for each of the languages, or we can have a separate wiki site (project) for each language! Let us explore the key comparisons between namespaces and projects:

Single project with multiple namespaces	Multiple projects with a single namespace
Content items are separated into multiple namespaces—for example, English contents are grouped in the English namespace, German contents are grouped in the German namespace, etc.	No need for multiple namespaces. Instead of creating multiple namespaces, multiple projects are created with a single namespace, which is the default Main namespace.
Main, Image, Help, User, User talk, and other namespaces are common to all namespaces under the project.	Main, Image, Help, User, User talk, and other namespaces are unique for each project. The namespaces of one project are not shared with other projects.
User contribution can be shown combined or separately for each namespace.	User contribution always shows separately for each project since there is no common namespace.
With multiple custom namespaces, we can use all the existing features in MediaWiki.	A few features in MediaWiki cannot be used across projects. They include (but are not limited to): Detection of linked pages Related changes What links here Use of templates Use of categories Message alert User contributions are always separate for separate projects Searching

Moving a Page

So far we have learned about creating new pages, editing them, and linking with other pages. What we have not discussed so far is how to move a page, rename it, or even delete it. When we are working with large amounts of content, it is inevitable that we might need to change the names of a few pages, move them to a new location, or delete unnecessary pages. The process is known as **moving** a page. There can be a lot of reasons why we need to move a page:

- For some reason (say by mistake) we may have entered the wrong title for a page. After creation of the page, we decide to change it, and so, we need to move the page rather than create a new page for the correct title.

- The scope of an article may have been reduced or extended, or a similar article may have been added in separately, and the new article may be more organized in comparison to the current one. So we need a page move here.

The terms "rename" and "move" mean the same in this context. They just refer to different models for performing the operation:

- **Rename:** Renaming keeps the page, but gives it another name. The page history of the previous page is now attached to the new name. A new page with the old name is created, which redirects to the new name and whose page history records the renaming.

- **Move**: This moves the contents and the page history to a new page; and changes the old page into a redirect. It also changes the page history into one that only records the renaming.

How to Make a Move

Every page in a namespace has a link named **move** at the top of the page beside the **history** tab. In order to see this feature, we have to log in to the site. When we click the **move** link, we will be taken to a special page named "move page". The page will have a few messages letting us know all the things we have discussed right now. The bottom of the page contains a small form that has two fields and a checkbox on it. The first field on the form is the new name for the page. The second one is the reason for which a move is being made. It is used to provide a better understanding for the administrators who can trace the move. The last option is the checkbox that says **Move talk page as well, if applicable**. Based on our requirement, we can check or uncheck the box and save the page to make the move. We are done; we have moved our old page to a new one.

The associated talk page, if any, will be automatically moved along with moving the page itself *unless*:

- You are moving the page across namespaces
- A non-empty talk page already exists under the new name
- You uncheck the checkbox

Even though the pages in all namespaces have a **move** link, a page can not be moved if it is in the Image or Category namespace. To change the name of an image, one needs to upload it again, and copy the image description. The only way to move a category page is to manually change all category tags that link to the category, and copy the editable part. There is no automatic way to move a category page in the manner one moves an article page.

One other type of pages that we cannot move are the **protected** pages, which are protected by administrators. If a page is protected from moves only, the **Move this page** link will not be available. In this case, we can ask that an administrator move it for us, or we can manually move the page, by copying the contents to a new page and redirecting the old page to the new page. Pages that are protected from editing are automatically protected from moves.

Undo a Move

It is sometimes required that a move be reverted. Sometimes a user may have moved the page without any reason or with a bad purpose. This type of thing happens in large projects, and in order to rectify this situation, we can always undo a move.

Normally, to undo a move from Page One to Page Two, simply:

1. Move Page Two back to Page One.
2. Request an administrator to delete Page Two.

If Page One has subsequently been edited, or the move software is behaving weirdly, only an administrator can sort things out:

1. Delete Page One.
2. Move Page Two to Page One.
3. Delete Page Two.

Swapping Two Pages

Think about a large project where we have many similar articles. It is very easy for users to enter information in a *similar* article rather than the *desired* article. In this case, the page swapping concept can come in handy to swap two similar pages or if required a totally different pair of pages. Those of us who are familiar with the swapping concept widely used in the field of computing, "swapping two variables using a third variable", can find it pretty straightforward. But for others it might sound new. What we do is simply use a third page to make the swap.

Suppose we want to move Page One to Page Two with history, and use Page Three as the temporary page for swapping, the process would be as follows:

1. Move Page One to Page Three (previously non-existent).
2. Request the administrator to delete Page One.
3. Move Page Two to Page One (this is allowed since Page One is deleted).
4. Request the administrator to delete Page Two.
5. Move Page Three to Page Two (this is allowed since Page Two is deleted).
6. Request the administrator to delete Page Three.

And we are done! The two pages have been swapped. Though the process is little bit lengthy, it is an effective way of swapping pages.

Look at the following image for a better understanding of the swapping procedure.

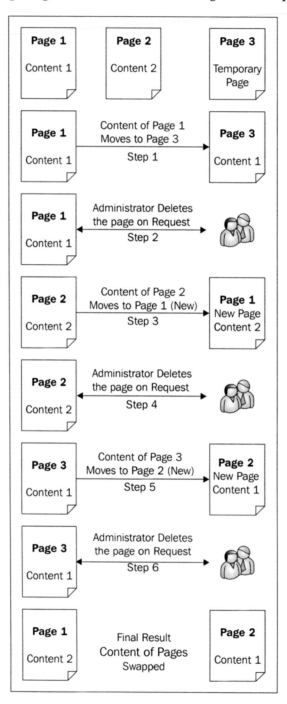

Special Pages

As the name suggests, special pages are used for special purposes, to make our site navigation and searching easier. We are discussing special pages so late in the chapter—after having covered categories, links, templates, etc.—as without understanding these terms properly, some of the concepts wouldn't make any sense to us. There are a lot of special pages in MediaWiki, and for all users, these pages are common. For sysops, however, there is a different set of special pages, which we will discuss in the *Administrating MediaWiki* chapter.

Special pages are created during installation on system demand. Note, however, that any new page can be added to the Special namespace, the namespace under which all special pages are listed. From our previous discussion earlier in this chapter, we also know that special pages do not have any corresponding talk pages. In order to view all the pages under special pages, click the **Special pages** link from the **toolbox** navigation area from the left of the screen or append Special:Specialpages to the URL to view the list. There are many special pages, and the list grows with each update of the MediaWiki software. We will discuss a few of the important and useful special pages here. First we will see a few basic special pages, and then move on to user-related special pages.

All Pages

The first of the special pages is the link for **All Pages**. This page lists all the pages in the wiki. By default, it shows all the pages under the Main namespace when the page is loaded. The pages are loaded in alphabetic order, and we can choose any namespace to load all the pages under that namespace. We can also filter the listed page with the starting character of the title. If we filter with the character E in the Main namespace, then all the page titles starting with A, B, C, and D will be discarded from the display, and all titles starting with E as well as letters after E will be shown. Before trying to create a page, it is always a good practice to check whether a page already exists from the list for a particular namespace.

Categories

This page lists all the available categories of the site with the number of pages under each category. This page helps us to find the available categories very easily.

File List

This page shows a list of uploaded images, which can be sorted by date, name, and size. Usually the files are listed with their name, file sizes, names of the users who have uploaded the file (or IP addresses from which the files have been uploaded), and the time of upload.

Popular Pages

This page shows the most popular or most viewed pages in the descending order of their popularity. With the help of this page, we can easily figure out which pages of the site are generating more interest in the visitors, and we can use that as an input to improve the overall site quality.

Create an Account or Login

This page is used for new users' registration and for existing users' login. We have already seen one example of this page in Chapter 4, where we created our first login. From this page, we can also retrieve our forgotten password.

Preferences

This page is used to set user preferences for the site. Each user can set his or her own preferences with the help of this page. In order to access this page, you need to log in first.

My Watchlist

You can always monitor or observe a certain page (or pages) if you wish to. You can mark a page and can visit it later or set it as your preferred page so that when someone alters the page, you get notified about the change. This is known as **watching** a page, which we will discuss in the next chapter. This page shows all the pages that you are watching, and requires you to login first.

User List

This page lists all registered users of the site sorted alphabetically. You can click on a username to visit that user's profile page.

List of Blocked IP Addresses and Usernames

This page lists all the blocked IP addresses and usernames for the wiki. Most of the time, admins block IP addresses and usernames to stop vandalism in the site.

Export Pages

This page is used to produce an XML file containing the wiki text and metadata of either the current version or of all revisions of one or more pages, specified in the form of a list; the XML file is in the format required for `Special:Import`. Exporting is typically done either in preparation for applying the latter at another MediaWiki project, or for searching within old page revisions. To export pages, you have to enter the titles in the textbox, one title per line, and select whether you want the current version as well as all old versions, with the page history lines, or just the current version with the info about the last edit.

Summary

We have learned techniques of organizing and managing our content, and have seen the use of categories, namespaces, and templates for organizing content better. We also discussed moving a page and swapping two page contents with history, and the use of special pages for specific purposes.

Things are really easy in MediaWiki. So far our focus has been on working with a single user. Now let us shift our focus to a multi-user environment, where there will be hundreds or thousands of visitors in a site performing different activities together. We will learn more about securing content and preventing vandalism in our next chapter.

6
MediaWiki in a Multi-User Environment

So far we have covered everything necessary for working with MediaWiki. We know about starting new pages and putting them into categories. We have used the login option once, when we were trying to upload files. We know that a wiki is a collaborative environment. This means we may have multiple users accessing the system every now and then. The count might be more than few thousands for a given moment if the site is popular. Each user can have different preferences and styles for viewing the content, and works on a shared file, which means conflicts can easily arise in such situations. In this chapter, we will take a detailed look at these issues. We will discuss:

- Disadvantages of having a completely open system
- Advantages of user accounts
- Setting up user accounts
- Customizing user accounts
- Finding out who has done what and when
- Considerations for a multi-user environment
- Resolving problems by reverting changes and solving edit conflicts
- Communicating with others

Disadvantages of Completely Open Systems

Keep in mind that not all users have good intentions. Since the system is open, anyone—including malicious users with bad intentions—can perform any activity on the site. An open system can face a lot of user-related problems. The first major problem is that anyone can edit or add contents. This can be dangerous if the added content is not legal and also if it is copyrighted. Since the user cannot be tracked, the site has to take the responsibility for such acts. Another major attack can be on the content itself—people with bad intentions can change content without any reason or present false information. Vandalism is also a common occurrence on such sites.

Advantages of User Accounts

If the site is protected by privileged access, then it is obvious that the site will be more secure than an open system. Most of the privileged access is provided by having user accounts with different levels of **access type**. A user name separates one identity from those of other people. There are many advantages of user accounts and privileges; some advantages are:

- The system can be set such that adding, editing, and deleting content may be performed only by registered users who are logged in to the system.

- Users can set their preferences such as skins, time zones, file format, etc.

- User can be identified by a name rather than the IP address of the user's machine. So even if a single user accesses from multiple machines, he or she will be identified by his or her user name rather than IP addresses.

- User names are easier to remember than IP addresses.

- Users can have their personal profile pages based on their user account names, and this helps others to know about them.

- User accounts give more flexibility when accessing content. Sometimes an administrator may block an IP address in order to stop malicious users from vandalizing a site. However, if the IP address is shared between multiple users, then it is not very wise to block it as this would stop more than one person from accessing the site. However, if we block a user account instead, then other users from the same IP address can still access the system.

- Users can create their own preferences for articles and monitor different topics, and even get notified about certain changes to the site.

Setting Up User Accounts

In the last chapter we saw how to create user account in MediaWiki. If the system is enabled for new user registration, then anyone can register from the specified link at the top right corner of the page. From our discussion in the last chapter, we may assume that you have already created one user account. We will use the **ghosthunter** user account here. Now we have to log in to the system using our user name and password. Once we are logged in, we can customize our user account based on our preferences.

Customizing User Accounts

When you sign up for an account, you might want to customize the site by changing the view, data formats and other settings. MediaWiki lets you do a lot through your preferences, which are divided into a few groups. They are:

- User profile
- Skin
- Files
- Date format
- Time zone
- Editing
- Recent changes
- Watchlist
- Search
- Miscellaneous

With changes in the version of the software, the preferences can change too. However, these are the common preferences that you will find upon clicking **my preferences** on the top navigation panel once you are logged in. We will now look at each of the preference settings in detail.

User Profile

In the user profile section, each user can set his or her personal information, such as **Real name**, **E-mail**, **Nickname**, and **Raw signatures**. When you are in the user data section in the preference page, you will see three different subsections:

- General user information
- Password options
- Email settings

Here is the screenshot of the **User profile** from the preference settings:

In the general user information, you can enter your real name (optional). You can also enter your email address if you want. Even though providing an email address is optional, you *have to* provide one if you want notification on changes made to pages and your user talk page, or even on simple or minor edits (such as spelling change, missed words, etc.) made on your created or watch page. Later in this chapter we will learn more about major edits and minor edits.

Nickname is an optional field too. Sometimes you can use a user name that is not necessarily your real name. You can define your identity in your signature. If you provide your nickname, then your signature will show the nickname. If you keep this field blank, then your user name will be shown in your signature. Below the nickname box, you will find a checkbox related to raw signatures.

If **Raw signatures (without automatic link)** is unchecked, then:

- The software enters **[[User:Name|** in front of your nickname text, and **]]** after it.

- Any characters in your nickname that would otherwise constitute Wiki markup and HTML markup are escaped as HTML character entities. A nickname of **]] | [[User talk:Name|Talk** will thus produce a signature of **]] | [[User talk:Name|Talk**, which is probably not what you want.

If **Raw signatures (without automatic link)** is checked, then:

- Nothing is added to the text that you specify. What you specify is what is used between the two dashes and the timestamp.

- Wiki markup and HTML markup are not escaped, allowing you to include links, font tags, images, and templates in your signature.

You can choose your preferred language from the **Language** setup option, and can also change your password. In order to change your current password, you have to enter your current password once and the new password twice in the respective boxes. In order to log in automatically every time you visit the site, you can check the box with label **Remember across sessions**.

Also, as we just discussed, email address setup is optional for all the users, but if you want to perform any of the following tasks, then you have to provide the email address:

- Receive an email notification when a change is made to pages you are monitoring or watching

- Get an email notification when your user talk page is changed

- Get email notifications when anyone makes minor edits to your pages

- Receive emails from other users

In order to access these features, your email address must first be authenticated by the system. If the email address is not authenticated, then you will see a message about the authentication process. Just below the message, a link named **Confirm your e-mail address** will be shown. Upon clicking the link, you will be taken to the confirmation page, where you will be required to click the button **Mail a confirmation code**. This will send a confirmation email to the address you have provided. Follow the link in the email to activate the email address. You can also disable user emails if you do not want to not receive any emails from other users directly. Before leaving the screen, do not forget to click the **Save** button, or else nothing will be saved and you will not get the desired result.

Skin

A MediaWiki skin is the style in which a page is displayed.Different stylesheets are used in order to define skins, as it's not the body of the page that changes, but rather the HTML code. The default skin used is the MonoBook skin, which we have been viewing in our wiki site all this time. From the preference section, you can click the **Skin** option to show all the skins available for the site. You can preview the skins by clicking the preview link just beside each skin's name.

Choose your preferred skin and save the page using the **Save** button. By default, the following skins are available in MediaWiki after installation:

- Chick
- Cologne blue
- MonoBook
- MySkin
- Nostalgia
- Simple
- Classic

The major difference among the skins is the way of showing different content and links. Some links are shown in a larger font size, for example, and some are presented in a list. Sometimes even the alignment of the contents may be different in different skins.

So far in this book, we have used only one type of skin—MonoBook, the default one. Here are the screenshots of the six other default skins available in MediaWiki with our home page content:

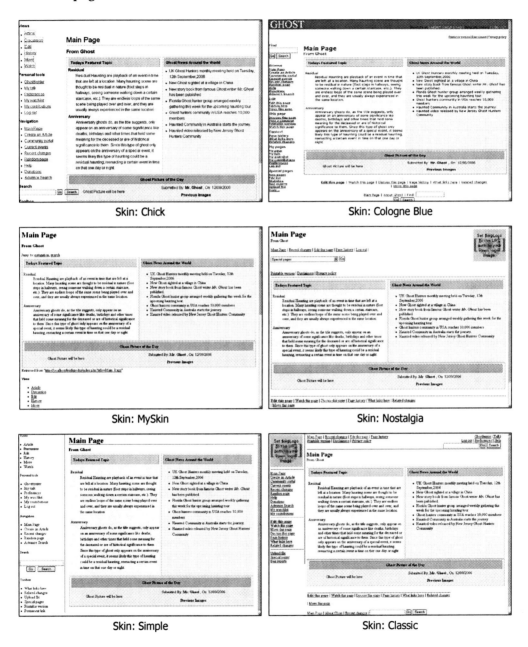

Skin: Chick

Skin: Cologne Blue

Skin: MySkin

Skin: Nostalgia

Skin: Simple

Skin: Classic

As you can see, the layout is different in each screen. So it is totally up to you to choose the skin you want. Also, if you want to make your own skin, that is possible with the help of CSS and HTML knowledge. We will look at this feature later on in this book.

Files, Date Format, and Time Zone Setup

We have created a gallery of images, and have displayed images in image pages. The display image and thumbnail image size can be defined in MediaWiki preferences.

We can also change date format according to our choice. We can set our local time zone by adding an offset value in the time-zone setup. The offset value is the number of hours to be added or subtracted from UTC to find your time zone. This time zone is used for calculating displayed page update timestamps.

Editing

Editing preferences let you set different editing options. Here are the available options:

Options	Summary
Rows, Columns	Here you can set up your preferred dimensions for the textbox used for editing page text.
Enable section editing via [edit] links	This option allows you to edit a section of content by clicking the edit links just beside the section header. If this option is disabled, then the section-edit link will not be shown to you.
Enable section editing by right clicking on section titles	This option requires JavaScript to be enabled in the browser. If this option is selected then right-clicking the section title will take you to the section edit page.
Edit pages on double click	This option also requires JavaScript enabled in the browser. On double-clicking anywhere on the page, you will be taken to the edit page if the option is enabled.
Edit box has full width	If this box is checked, the edit box (when you click **Edit this page**) will be as wide as the browser window minus the quickbar width.
Show edit toolbar	A toolbar with editing buttons will be displayed in compatible browsers.
Show preview on first edit	When pressing the **edit** button or otherwise following a link to an edit page, show not only the edit box but also the rendered page, just as after pressing **Show preview**.

Options	Summary
Show preview before edit box	If you select this option, a preview will be displayed above the edit box when you click the **Show preview** button while editing a page.
Add pages I Add to my watchlist	If this option is selected, any pages that you create will be automatically added to your watchlist.
Add pages I edit to my watchlist	If this option is selected, any pages that you modify will be automatically added to your watchlist.
Mark all edits minor by default	This option automatically selects the **This is a minor edit** checkbox when you edit pages.
Use external editor by default	Changes editing from online version to external program.
Use external diff by default	Changes differing from online version to external program.
Prompt me when entering a blank edit summary	If you enable this option, and after editing any content if you do not put any edit summary in the edit summary box and you try to save it, then you will be prompted to enter the summary of the edit and then save.

Other Preferences

You may select the number of changes that will be shown by default on the Recent changes and Watchlist page. Once on those pages, links are provided for other options. You may choose to mark edits as being **minor** (meaning fixes too trivial for trusting users to check up on). It applies to recent changes and enhanced recent changes, but not to the watchlist. The **Enhanced recent changes** option is currently not supported by all browsers. It shows grouped recent changes per day by article, displays the titles of the changed articles in an order (from the latest change to the oldest), or in the case of hiding minor edits, the latest major change. This feature applies also to related changes, but not to the watchlist.

For search page preferences, you can set up the number of results that will be shown on a single search page. The **Lines per hit** option is little confusing. If you put a number x in the field, then it will search for the contents of the search field through x number of lines starting from the article. Any occurrence of the search text after x lines will not be shown. You can also choose your searchable namespaces from the list of namespaces. By default only the **Main** namespace is checked. You can check any namespace for the search domain.

In the miscellaneous preference setup, you can set broken links to be an internal link to a non-existing page that has an automatic link to the edit page. Normally, link text will be underlined. Optionally, you may request that links not be underlined, although your browser may not respect this setting. **Hover box over wiki links** shows the title in little hover box when a mouse cursor hovers over the link. Some browsers show link URL instead of the title in the hover box. **Auto number headings** will add hierarchical outline-style numbering to headers in articles. One interesting option in this section is the showing of a table of content if the number of headers is more than three. By default the option is checked, and that's why we are able to generate a table of contents for our site. If we uncheck this option, the table of contents will not be generated automatically.

> After saving, you may have to bypass your browser's cache to see the changes.
>
> **Mozilla / Firefox / Safari**: Hold down *Shift* while clicking **Reload**, or press *Ctrl+Shift+R* (*Cmd+Shift+R* on Apple Mac).
>
> **IE**: Hold *Ctrl* while clicking **Refresh**, or press *Ctrl+F5*.
>
> **Konqueror**: Simply click the **Reload** button, or press *F5*.
>
> **Opera**: Completely clear their cache in **Tools | Preferences**.

Finding Out Who Has Done What and When

Each page except special pages contains a history of all the changes made to that page. This is known as the page history, though it can also be called edit history. It consists of the old versions of the wiki text, as well as a record of the date and time of every edit, the user name or IP address of the user who wrote it, and their edit summary. This history tool can be used to track changes very easily. You can access the page history by clicking the **history** tab at the top of the page. Page history is the most suitable option for tracking changes related to the page. We can also revert changes from the history. So, understanding page history structure is important in order to better utilize the option.

Edits are shown from newest to oldest. Each edit takes up one line, which shows time and date, the contributor's name or IP, and the edit summary, as well as other diagnostic information. Let's have a look at some of the functions of this page:

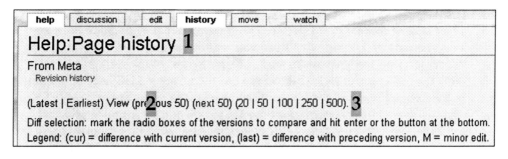

1. At the top we have the page name, which stays the same as that for the page title, except that the **history** tab of the top navigation is highlighted.

2. After that we have pagination information for the listings. These links take you to the most recent edits (**Latest**), oldest edits (**Earliest**), or the next or previous page of edits (**next n** or **previous n**, where **n** can be set by clicking the number within brackets on the right side, which we will cover next. By default the value of **n** is **50**, as shown in the image). Note that the black text in brackets will become links, when applicable.

3. The blue numbers list the number of edits displayed on a page: **20, 50, 100, 250**, or **500**. A higher number increases the length of a page but reduces the number of pages; the number you select replaces **n** in the links to the previous or next pages.

4. Next we focus on the actual listing. The first item on the listing is **(cur)**. This takes you to a **diff page**, a page where the difference between two versions of the page is shown, showing the difference between that edit and the current version. The current revision appears below the changes, so you can see how the page is now rendered.

5. **(last)** takes you to a diff page showing the changes between that edit and the previous version. The later version (the one on the same line as the last you clicked on) appears below the changes; so you can see how the page was rendered.

6. The two columns of radio buttons can be used to select and compare any two versions of the page. Let's say you want to compare the versions corresponding to numbers **10** and **11** (refer to the following figure). First, click the left-column radio button next to the number **11**. The right column is then populated with buttons till the row before the number **11**. Click the right-column button next to number **10**. Finally click **Compare selected versions**. This takes you to a diff page showing the changes between the two versions. The more recent version (in this case, number **10**) appears below the changes; so you can see how the page was rendered.

7. After the radio box, we have a time and date listed, which give the time and date of the edit.

8. The user name or IP address of the contributor appears just after the date and time field.

9. This is the edit summary. It is the text the user wrote in the edit summary box (below the edit box, if you recall).

10. This edit summary begins with an arrow link and gray text. This means that the user has only edited a section of the page (shown in the gray text). This text is automatically added when you edit a section. A standard edit summary can be added by the user. This appears in black text.

11. **m** stands for minor edit (small corrections to a page). These help you understand the type of changes that have been made.

What Must be Considered for Multi-User Environments?

One day Mr. Ghost Writer found that his article has been changed. Someone changed article but he could not figure out the change since the article is a long one. The person might have changed the names of the characters of the story, or may have deleted random lines from the story. So Ghost Writer panics. How will he figure out the changes? How will he know who has done the changes? How can he revert changes to get the original content? There are a lot of questions like these inside Ghost Writer's mind. Can we help him out from the situation?

Though the above story is not such a frequent one, it is quite common in a collaborative site, and can turn into your own story. All users have different intentions. Among them, we might have some malicious users who want to perform only harmful activities on the site—hackers for one example, vandals being another. Apart from these, there are some novice users, who do things unintentionally (the damage *is* done, though), but without their noticing. Everyday we have to deal with a situation like this on a wiki site. This is quite common when we have given permission to users to edit content. So as a user we have to be careful of such incidents, as a popular wiki site can have thousands of users accessing (and trying to change the content for) the same page at a given time.

If we are careful and follow some common rules, then we can overcome this type of situation to occur. Here are few rules that we need to follow:

- Look for recent changes before you change anything
- Watch the page
- Analyze the page difference
- Provide an edit summary when you change the page
- Mark the edit as minor if changes are not significant
- Mark edits as patrolled

Look for Recent Changes before you Change Anything

A recent changes page gives you the whole list of changes made in the wiki site. It gives you a listing of newly added pages, changes and edits, reverted pages with history, differences, and a lot of other options. Using this page, users can monitor and review the work of other users, and this allows mistakes to be corrected and vandalism to be eliminated. There is a link to the recent changes page at the top of each page and in the sidebar of each page.

You can also create a link to the page as **[[Special:Recentchanges]]**. Recent changes pages look like the following:

```
special page

Recent changes

Track the most recent changes to the wiki on this page.

Below are the last 50 changes in the last 7 days, as of 22:25, 19 January 2007.
Show last 50 | 100 | 250 | 500 changes in last 1 | 3 | 7 | 14 | 30 days
Hide minor edits | Show bots | Hide anonymous users | Hide logged-in users | Hide patrolled edits | Hide my edits
Show new changes starting from 22:25, 19 January 2007
Namespace:  all          [v]  [ Go ]  [] Invert selection

19 January 2007

  ▪ (diff) (hist) . . N A night in the jungle; 22:25 . . 127.0.0.1 (Talk) (New story page)
  ▪ (diff) (hist) . . The Haunting; 21:04 . . 127.0.0.1 (Talk)
  ▪ (diff) (hist) . . The Haunting; 21:03 . . 127.0.0.1 (Talk)
  ▪ (diff) (hist) . . The Haunting; 21:00 . . 127.0.0.1 (Talk)

16 January 2007

  ▪ (diff) (hist) . . Test10; 23:21 . . Admin (Talk | contribs)
  ▪ (Upload log); 23:18 . . Admin (Talk | contribs) (uploaded "Image.11ff.jpg")
```

The previous images shows recent changes occurred on two days. Let us describe what each entry means, from left to right:

- The first thing on the list is a **diff** link. **diff** links to the diff page for this edit; it is not available for new pages, or for page moves.
- The **hist** link corresponds to the **page history** on the edited page; it shows not just this edit but also older and newer ones. For page moves, the **hist** link leads to the history of the new page title.
- A bold **m** indicates that the user marked the edit **minor**. Only logged-in users can mark an edit as minor, to avoid abuse.
- A bold **N** indicates that the page is **new**. It is possible for a change to possess both the minor and new indicators; this is typically used for new redirects.
- A bold **!** indicates that the page is **unpatrolled**. We will focus on patrolled and unpatrolled edits at the end of this chapter.
- The next link is a link to the current version of the page.
- Next is the time in UTC format. You can change the time to your timezone using the preferences that we have just learned.
- For logged-in users, the next link is a link to their user home page. For users who are not logged in, the link points to their user contributions.

- The final link points to the user's talk page.
- When we do a page move, a link is provided for the old as well as the new title after the user talk link in **Recent changes**.

We can also filter our recent changes list with the options provided in the page. We can hide minor edits from being shown in the recent changes list. We can also hide patrolled edit and logged-in-user information. We can filter the changed list by namespace. We can also choose the number of edits and days for the recent change list.

It is always important and good practice to go through the recent changes page in order to view latest changes made to the site. The topic you are going to add may be found there. Maybe somebody else has just added that; you can reduce redundancy here. You can also view the list to check if any page has been changed.

Watch the Page

Though recent changes list all the changed files in the site, this is not a good way of finding changes made on your edits. If the size of the site is big, then it is almost impossible to find all the changes made to your edits or to pages that you created. MediaWiki has a wonderful feature to solve this problem. It is called watching a page. You can watch any page you want. If you watch a page, that page will be added to your watchlist. When the page has been changed, edited, or added to, you will get an automatic notification from the system based on your preference setting (such as email on page change). Also, on your watchlist page, all the pages that have been modified since your last visit will be shown in bold, so you can easily identify the changes. In order to list a page on your watchlist, click the **watch** option just above the page title. When you visit the page again, there will be an **unwatch** link instead of **watch**, which is used to remove the page from your watchlist.

Analyzing the Page Difference

A **diff** is the difference between two versions of a page, and can be viewed from the page history. For every version, there are potentially two radio buttons: the left column is for selecting the older version, the right column for selecting the newer one. Pressing **Compare selected versions** gives the difference between the two versions. So if you know that someone *has* changed the content, you can definitely view *what* actually has been changed by the user. This is a great option for reverting changes with proper understanding of the made changes.

Here is an example of a difference page:

| article | discussion | edit | history | move | watch |

The Haunting 69

(Difference between revisions)

| Revision as of 21:49, 19 January 2007 (edit) | Current revision (21:49, 19 January 2007) (edit) (undo) |
| 127.0.0.1 (Talk) | 127.0.0.1 (Talk) |

← Previous diff

Line 1:

- {{Movie_Summary

- |The Haunting

Line 1:

+ {{Movie_Summary|The Haunting| Myposter.jpg |The Haunting DVD cover|[[Robert Wise]]|[[Robert Wise]]

+ |'''Novel:'''
[[Shirley Jackson]]|[[Nelson Gidding]]|[[Julie Harris]]
[[Richard Johnson]]
[[Claire Bloom]]|[[MGM]]|[[September 18]], [[1963]] ([[USA]])|112 min.|[[English language|English]]|}}

For special cases, such as the diff for a single edit or a diff between an old and the current version, other possibilities are clicking **cur** or **last** in the page history or on the recent changes page. The diff is also shown during an edit conflict so you can see exactly what you need to reintegrate.

When you view the difference, the two versions are shown side by side. In the old version, paragraphs that differ are yellow, and in the new version, they are green. In left-to-right languages, the old version is on the left. This layout is reversed in right-to-left scripts. Text removed from a paragraph is shown in red in the old version, and new text within a paragraph is shown in red in the new version. If a whole paragraph was removed or added, the text is not red but just black, while the other side is blank (white). Unchanged text is black on gray, and is shown only in part, before and after the changed text.

The diff shows differences per line. Some editors find that adding manual line breaks improves the diff function. As well as showing the difference between versions, the diff page has links to the user pages and talk pages of the users who edited both the last and current versions. Links to the users' contribution lists are also shown. For sysops, a **rollback** button is shown, allowing them to revert from the new version to the old one.

Note, however, that this is even shown when viewing the diff between the recent version of a page and a version older than the last version by an author other than the one of the most current version, in which case the rollback would not undo the change that is displayed. Thus, if user A vandalized a page and user B partially reverted that vandalism, the diff of the two together shows the remaining vandalism, but rollback reverts the partial repair by user B. Edit summaries are also shown on the diff page. These appear in the row beneath the user names. If the user has used links in their edit summary, these act as links on the diff page as well.

Provide Edit Summary when you Change the Page

When you edit an article, you can see a small field labeled **Summary** under the main edit-box. It looks like the image below. This is known as the edit summary. It is highly recommended that one fill in the edit summary field, as it makes it easier for you and your fellow contributors to understand what has changed, and is helpful when going through the history of the page.

Summary:

"Something is better than nothing" is an axiom well known to all of us. This is true when you are editing in MediaWiki. *Always* fill in the summary field. This is considered an important guideline. Even a short summary is better than no summary. An edit summary is even more important if you delete any text. Also, mentioning one change and not another can be misleading, especially to someone to whom the other one is more important; add "and misc." to cover the other change(s).

Accurate summaries help people decide whether it is worthwhile for them to check a change. We've found that summaries often pique the interest of contributors with expertise in the area. This may not be as necessary for "minor changes", but even then, a summary like "fixed spelling" would be nice.

The edit summary box can hold one line of 200 characters. If you attempt to paste more than this, only the first 200 characters will be displayed—the rest will be disregarded. In the case of a small addition to an article, it is highly recommended the full text of this addition be copied to the **Summary** field, giving a maximum of information with a minimum of effort. This way, readers of the summary will be unlikely to check the page itself as they already know the extent of the edit. These kinds of summaries allow users to check recent changes, page history, and user contributions very efficiently. This also reduces load on the servers.

In addition to a summary of the change itself, the **Summary** field may also contain an explanation of the change; note that if the reason for an edit is not clear, it is more likely to be reverted, especially in the case that some text is deleted. To give a longer explanation, use the talk page and make a note about it in the edit summary.

After saving the page, the summary can not be edited—another reason to avoid spelling errors.

The edit summary appears in black italics format in the following places:

- **Page history**: List of changes to the page you edited
- **User contributions**: List of all your edits
- **Diff page**: Shows the difference between two edits
- **List of new pages**: Shows the edit summary of the creation

The following locations show edit summary of the last edit only:

- **Watchlist**: List of recent changes to watched pages (logged-in users only)
- **Recent changes**: List of all recent edits
- **Wikipedia IRC channels**: Real-time list of all edits
- **Related changes**: List of recent changes to pages linked to the page you edited

When applying the section-editing feature, the section title is automatically inserted as the initial version or first part of the edit summary. Put more details after this text. If you provide a long summary yourself, you can delete the section title in order to stay within the limit of 200 characters. When inserting a section by applying section editing on the section before or after it, delete the automatic edit summary to avoid confusion.

File Upload Summary

When uploading an image, you can supply an upload summary. This serves multiple purposes, and can serve as:

- A second part of the automatically created edit summary of the upload log (the first part giving the file name)
- Text in the entry of the image history
- If the file name of the image is new, the upload summary can also serve as:
  - An edit summary for the creation of the image page
  - Wikitext for the editable part of the image page, which includes the following possibilities: briefly describing the image, providing internal or external links, calling templates, specifying one or more categories that the image falls under

The capacity of the upload summary is one line of 250 characters; in the upload log, the last part may fall off, because this can contain at most 255 characters, including **uploaded "filename"** (where **filename** stands for the name of the uploaded image).

Mark Edit as Minor if Changes are Not Significant

When editing a page, logged-in users may mark a change to a page as a minor edit. It is often a matter of personal judgment, but generally implies trivial changes only, such as typo corrections, formatting, and presentational changes, such as rearranging of text without changing any content. The checkbox to denote an edit as minor is shown at the bottom of the edit page, as circled in the following image:

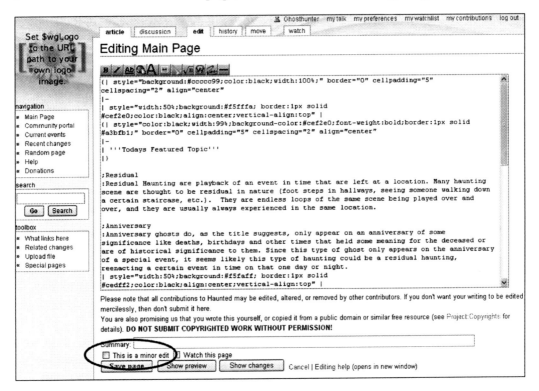

By contrast, a major edit makes the article worth reviewing for anyone who watches it closely. Therefore, any change that affects the meaning of an article is not minor, even if it involves one word.

The distinction between major and minor edits is significant because you may decide to ignore minor edits when viewing recent changes; logged-in users can even set their preferences to not display such edits. No one wants to be fooled into ignoring a significant change to an article simply because it was marked minor, of course. So remember to consider the opinions of other editors when choosing this option.

Users who are not logged into the wiki are not permitted to mark changes as minor because of the potential for vandalism. The ability to mark changes as minor is another reason to register.

It is always better to mark the edit as minor if you are doing the following changes:

- Spelling corrections
- Simple formatting (capitalization, bold, italics, etc.)
- Formatting that does not change the meaning of the page (for example, adding horizontal lines, or splitting a paragraph into two where such splitting isn't contentious)
- Obvious factual errors (changing 1873 to 1973, where the event in question clearly took place in 1973)
- Fixing layout errors

We have to remember the following things when we are marking an edit as minor edit:

- Any change to the source text, wikitext, even if it does not affect the presentation of the page in HTML (if it involves adding a space or a line break, for example) will still be treated as a change according to the database.
- Marking a major change as a minor one is considered bad manners, especially if the change involves the deletion of some text.
- Reverting pages is not likely to be considered minor under most circumstances. When the status of a page is disputed, and particularly if an edit war is brewing, then it's better not to mark any edit as minor. Reverting blatant vandalism is an exception to this rule.
- A user's watchlist will only list the most recent change made to a page, even if that edit was minor. Therefore, a minor change will supersede a major one in the watchlist. This is because a user who keeps a watchlist is generally interested in all changes made to a page. If you are uncertain about the changes made to a page, double-check the page history.
- If you accidentally mark an edit as minor when it was in fact a major edit, you should make a second "dummy" edit, but make a note in the edit summary that "the previous edit was major". As a trivial edit to be made for this purpose, just opening the edit box and saving (changing nothing) will not work, neither will adding a blank space at the end of a line or a blank line at the end of the page—in these cases the edit is canceled and its summary discarded. However, one can, for example, add an extra space between two words, or can even add a line break. These changes are preserved in the wikitext and recorded as a change, although they do not change the rendered page.

- It may be worth communicating any disagreement about what is minor via **Talk** or a message to the contributor, being careful to avoid a flame war with other users. There is a gray area here, and many contributors will appreciate feedback on whether they've got it right.

It is also good to remember the following terms since we are using these terms every now and then:

- **Dummy edit**: A dummy edit is a change in wikitext that has little or no effect on the rendered page, but saves a useful dummy edit summary. The dummy edit summary can be used for text messaging, and correcting a previous edit summary such as an accidental marking of a previous edit as "minor". Text messaging via the edit summary is a way of communicating with other editors. Text messages may be seen by dotted IP number editors who don't have a user talk page, or editors who haven't read the subject's talk page, if it exists. Each edit summary can hold 202 text characters. A dummy edit should be checked as "minor" by logged-in editors.

  Example:

  ◦ Changing the number of newlines in the edit text such as putting a newline where no newline exists or adding one more newline to two existing newlines has no effect on the rendered page. But changing from one newline to two newlines makes a rendered difference as it creates spacing between the contents in Mediawiki and may not be a dummy edit. Adding newlines to the end of the article will not save as a dummy edit.

- **Null edit**: A null edit occurs if a page save is made when the wikitext is not changed, which is useful for refreshing the cache. A null edit will not record an edit, make any entry in the page history, in recent changes, etc., and the edit summary is discarded.

  Examples:

  ◦ Opening the edit window and saving.

  ◦ Adding newlines only to the end of the article and saving is also a null edit.

Patrolled Edit

This is a new feature of MediaWiki starting from version 1.4. Patrolling edits is a way to verify that they are good edits, and to collaborate on filtering spam and vandalism. If you're combing through the recent changes list, and you look at an article that is good, you can mark it as "patrolled" so that other users know that it is good. After clicking **diff** on a change in a recent changes page, you may see a link **Mark as patrolled**, similar to the one shown in the following image:

If you don't see this option, then the option is not enabled for you. Patrolled edits are restricted to administrators in most MediaWiki projects.

Policies may vary among projects whether an article can be marked as patrolled if it is not obvious vandalism, or only when the correctness has been verified.

In the recent changes page, an unpatrolled edit will look like this (note the ! mark before the title for each diff):

However, a patrolled edit would look like the following one (look at the circled entry, where no ! mark is shown):

Reverting Changes

Sometimes we might need to revert a page if someone has changed the page's content without any reason, wrongly, or, of course, for a bad purpose. To stop such activities and get back our actual content, we can always revert changes made to our page. To **revert** is to undo all changes made after a certain time. The result will be that the page becomes identical to how it used to be at some previous time. A **partial revert** undoes only some of those changes. In order to revert a page, you need to take the following steps:

1. Go to the page you are reverting, click on **history** at the top to move into page history, and click on the time and date of the earlier version to which you wish to revert.

2. When that page comes up, you'll see something like (**Revision as of 22:19 Aug 15, 2005**) below the title.

3. Verify that you've selected the correct version, and click to **edit** the page, as you would normally. Remember: in case of vandalism, take the time to make sure that you are reverting to the last version without the vandalism; there may be multiple vandal edits.

4. You'll get a warning, above the edit box, about editing an out-of-date revision.

5. After heeding the warning, save the page. Be sure to add the word **revert** and a brief explanation for the revert to the edit summary. Some users abbreviate **revert** as **rv**. A useful addition is to link the user names associated with the versions you are reverting from and to. For example, a good edit summary would be:

   rv edits by 127.0.0.1 to last version by Ghost Writer

6. The clickable links are created by entering **[[User:Username | RealName]]** (replacing **Username** with the real IP address or user name for logged-in users, and replacing **RealName** with their real user name).

7. Click on **history** again. A new line will have been added, and you'll be able to verify (by clicking on **last**) that you un-did the vandalism plus all subsequent bona fide edits, if any, which you are responsible for redoing.

> In a vandalism case where sections of text were simply deleted and then subsequent edits were made by others, it may be easier for you to cut and paste those missing sections of text back in, than to revert and then redo the edits.

Check the contribution history of the user who vandalized the article. Click on their IP address or user name. Clicking on their IP will often bring you directly to their user contribution page. If you are able to click on their user name, that will bring you to their user page. In the lower left-hand corner, there is a toolbox with a **User contributions** link. Click that. If this user is vandalizing many articles, report them to sysops.

Resolving Edit Conflict

Mr. Ghost Writer is editing his story "The ghost of the mathematician". At the same time, Mr. Dracula found a few spelling mistakes in the story, and he is also editing the page. Mr. Dracula finishes his editing and saves the page; so the page has a new version. Now when Mr. Ghost Writer, who has edited a lot in the article, tries to save, he gets a message citing an **edit conflict**!

This is a very common case for any wiki site, where we have multiple users accessing the same content. This situation arises every now and then in collaborative environments. We gave example of two users, but this can occur for more than two users. Suppose 10 users are editing the page at the same time. What will happen, and how should the edit conflict be resolved?

When an edit conflict takes place, the edit conflict page is shown with the conflict page source. The first text area shows your wiki text or source. After that it shows differences in the two edits with the **diff** option. After that, the other edit option is shown in the next text area. If you save your changes using the **Save** button, then the other changes will be gone. So before saving any of the changes, we have to merge both the sources (yes we have to merge since the process is not automatic).

In our example, Dracula made small changes, but Ghost Writer made big changes, so it will be fine if Ghost Writer works on his text area, makes changes where Dracula changed the content, and then both of the edits are merged. It is always helpful if anyone's edit is minor. If the situation was reverse, where Ghost Writer saves the page first and Dracula tried to save later, then Dracula would have received the edit-conflict error. Dracula can then work on Mr. Ghost Writer's work, since Ghost Writer has made the major changes. The situation will become complex if both have them have done major changes. Both Dracula and Ghost Writer have to do their best to solve this issue. It is suggested that the latter user who got the edit summary should view the difference section and change the contents accordingly.

Sometimes there are users who try to edit the contents in different editors rather than in the MediaWiki editor. They copy the content from the edit box, paste it to an editor, and close the edit box page in MediaWiki. After changing the content, they come back to the site and click **edit** again and replace the whole thing with their changes. If someone else has made changes in the meantime, these changes would get lost during the paste. So there is no edit conflict shown, even though there is a clear edit conflict. This is known as a **logical edit conflict**.

In order to avoid logical edit conflicts, users must follow the rules:

- Paste your changes to the same edit box that was originally copied from.

Or

- Check the page history before pasting your changes. If someone else has changed the page, then merge the current version with your changes and then save.

Because edit conflicts are irritating and time consuming, you may choose to alter your editing habits to render them less frequent—aiming to make edits to pages that have not been edited recently, such as those listed on ancient pages in the special namespace.

Another means of avoiding edit conflicts is to make a single large change, rather than frequent small changes; this makes it more likely that you will get an edit conflict, but less likely that you will cause others to get an edit conflict. Using the **Show preview** button helps here.

To reduce the chances of edit conflicts, you can use a notice like, "In Use, do not edit until 05:30 UTC", in the page for others when you are editing a page over a long period of time. So before starting the edit, make a minor change to the page with this type of message so that other people know someone is working on it.

Communicating with Other Users

Since we are working in a collaborative environment, it is always necessary to communicate with others properly and efficiently. The edit summary is a good way to let others know that what you have changed in an article. Also, marking a minor edit gives others an option to overlook the edit. However, these are indirect ways of communicating with other users. What about direct communication? Can we communicate directly to other users (such as by sending a message or inserting comments)?

MediaWiki has a very good feature called **talk page**, which can be used to communicate with others very efficiently. There are two types of talk pages: **standard talk pages** are used to discuss an article, while **user talk pages** are used to communicate with other users or leave them messages. Every page has an associated talk page, except pages in the **Special** namespace, which we already have discussed. If there is no discussion for a page, the link to its talk page will be red. You can still discuss the page—you will just be the first person to do so.

Making a Community Site with Talk Pages

Yes what you are reading is true. We can make a community site with talk pages. In a community site, we communicate with other users (such as in forums or blogs, where we make comments or reply on the topic). We can talk with a user as well as discuss a topic. MediaWiki gives us the option to implement both these features required for a community site. We can use a standard talk page for discussion on a particular article and the user talk page for communicating with users.

In order to comment on an article, you have to click on the **discussion** tab just above the article's title. That will take you to the talk page, where you can view all the entries. In order to add your say on the page, you have to click the **edit** link as you did when editing an article. This is the same as editing an article page, but we have to remember a few things when entering new entries:

- First of all, we should sign our contributions by typing three tildes or clicking the **signature** button from the **edit** toolbar. This will show the signature beside the comment and will also let others know who left the comment. If you do not do so, then leaving messages would be quite pointless, wouldn't it? We are talking about communicating with others and your identity is a required part of this communication.

- The second important thing is we have to format our discussion or comments properly. It is always good to show the depth of a message, but if you do not format the text yourself, then it will be shown in the same column. We need to format the conversation using different formatting techniques that we learned in the formatting section. The most useful one is the colon (:), which works as tab in the display. We can use a colon to show the depth of the message. Each colon represents a tab, and is commonly used in discussions on user and article talk pages. If a reply is made to a statement, one adds a colon to the number of colons used in the statement being replied to. This style of conversation is easier to read.

Take a look at the following examples, and you will find out why these two rules are important:

```
what was the name of the ghost? --[[User:WikiSysop|WikiSysop]] 22:14,
8 May 2006 (Central Asia Standard Time)

i think it was John -- [[User:Ghost]]

No i think it is David -- [[User:Mr. Dracula]]

which ghost ? -- [[User:Vampire]]

Are you out of your mind, vampire ? -- [[User:Witch]]

No i am not, but can you tell me which ghost name you want to
know -- [[User:Vampire]]

This is getting crazy (this is a bad comment since no signature
provided)
```

This will produce the following output:

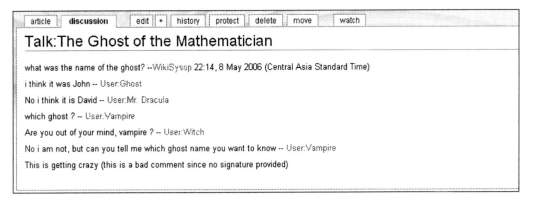

Can we find out which comment is for which reply? We can't, because all comments are in a single column i.e., none are indented. Also, at the end of the comment a user hasn't put his or her name—so we don't know who is getting the feeling that all this crazy! Now take a look at a well-formatted talk page:

```
what was the name of the ghost? --[[User:WikiSysop|WikiSysop]]

:i think it was John -- [[User:Ghost]]

:No i think it is David -- [[User:Mr. Dracula]]

:which ghost ? -- [[User:Vampire]]

::Are you out of your mind, vampire ? -- [[User:Witch]]

:::No i am not, but can you tell me which ghost name you want to
know -- [[User:Vampire]]

:Dracula, you are right -- [[User:WikiSysop|WikiSysop]]

my next question is what was the ghost formula written
by david? --[[User:WikiSysop|WikiSysop]]
: was it 1+2+3 = 6 ??? just kidding, dont know -- [[Vampire]]
```

This will produce the following output:

| article | **discussion** | edit | + | history | protect | delete | move | watch |

Talk:The Ghost of the Mathematician

what was the name of the ghost? --WikiSysop

    i think it was John -- User:Ghost

    No i think it is David -- User:Mr. Dracula

    which ghost ? -- User:Vampire

        Are you out of your mind, vampire ? -- User:Witch

            No i am not, but can you tell me which ghost name you want to know -- User:Vampire

    Dracula, you are right -- WikiSysop

my next question is what was the ghost formula written by david? --WikiSysop

    was it 1+2+3 = 6 ??? just kidding, dont know -- Vampire

You can see the difference for yourself. So always try to format your conversations, and also make some meaningful comment.

To access the user talk page, just click the user name in the user signature, and it will take you to the user talk page for that particular user. Now as with the general talk page you can edit the user talk page as well. Suppose someone enters a comment on your talk page or leaves a message. After your user talk page has been edited, the alert **You have new messages** is automatically displayed on all pages you view, until you view your user page.

Summary

In this chapter we learned about the disadvantages of an open system and advantages of user accounts. We have also learned how we can customize MediaWiki based on our preferences. We have learned about problems that can occur in the multi-user environment of a wiki site. We also learned about preventing such problems and resolving edit conflicts. We discussed how to create a discussion page and communicate with other users. So we know all aspects of creating a multi-user wiki site using MediaWiki. In the next chapter, we will start learning about administering MediaWiki, where we will require at least a little knowledge about PHP. So before you start the next chapter, have a review of your PHP knowledge.

7
Administrating MediaWiki

We have learned to use MediaWiki from a user's perspective. We know how to edit a page, link a page, put pages into categories, and communicate with others. All the functionalities that we have learned so far do not require any special privileges except for registering or logging in to the system. However, there are some functions that require some special administrative privileges. It is very common in today's web world that we have someone to configure and maintain a site for us. We call him or her a site administrator. In MediaWiki we have similar people with administrative access that we call Sysops or system operators. Their core job is to manage the site and configure different settings and perform administrative functions to keep the site live and running smoothly.

In this chapter, we will learn about the administrative functionalities available in MediaWiki. For this chapter, you will also need some knowledge about PHP for modifying files. So it will be great if you have some basic knowledge about PHP for changing few settings. If you do not have any knowledge about PHP, don't worry; as we go through examples, you will be able to pick up few basics of PHP. So here we go.

What You Show Know

Before knowing what we can do as admin, it is always important for us to know:

- What the architecture of the software is
- What the file structure in the installed server is
- Which are the files that are critical for configuration

We will learn all these things here. When we install MediaWiki on our server, all the files and folders are copied to the installation folder. In Chapter 2, we learned that after the installation process we have to move the LocalSettings.php file to the root folder from the /config folder. This is one major file for configuration.

We have another important configuration file, and that is the `DefaultSettings`. `php` file inside the `/includes` folder. Both of these files contain the configuration setup for MediaWiki. In order to ensure correct installation, we need to adjust those configuration properties based on our requirements.

Access Types

In the current version of MediaWiki, there are four types of users available. They are:

- General user
- Sysop
- Bureaucrat
- Bot

We've already learned about the general user—we have gone through the process of registering a new user and setting preferences for the user. We've also seen the sysop account, which we created during the installation process. Let us review the different user types and their access rights.

General User

This is the general user account created from the registration option in the wiki site. They can in general create new page, read articles, and edit them.

Sysop

This is the most common privileged user in MediaWiki. A user marked as 'sysop' can delete and undelete pages, protect and unprotect pages, block and unblock IPs, issue read-only SQL queries to the database, etc. A sysop is also known as the administrator or admin in Wikipedia and other wiki sites.

Bureaucrat

This is a higher-level access type than sysop. A bureaucrat can turn any user into a sysop.

Bot

This is a registered bot account. If edits are made by this account, then they will not appear by default in the recent changes list. This is intended for mass imports of data without flooding human edits from view.

There is another type of user available in MediaWiki known as a "developer". This access type is almost obsolete and will be removed in future MediaWiki versions. So we will not talk about this type of access.

Let's have a look at the default access chart for all user types:

Access Type	Non Registered User	User	Sysop	Bureaucrat	Bot
Read	Yes	Yes	Yes	Yes	Yes
Create page	Yes	Yes	Yes	Yes	Yes
Move	No	Yes	Yes	No	No
Edit	Yes	Yes	Yes	Yes	Yes
Create talk page	Yes	Yes	Yes	Yes	Yes
Delete	No	No	Yes	No	No
Protect	No	No	Yes	No	No
Block	No	No	Yes	No	No
User right	No	No	No	Yes	No
Create account	Yes	Yes	Yes	Yes	Yes
Upload	No	Yes	Yes	No	No
Reupload	No	Yes	Yes	No	No
Reupload Shared	No	Yes	Yes	No	No
Rollback	No	No	Yes	No	No
Patrol	No	No	Yes	No	No
Edit interface	No	No	Yes	No	No
Bot	No	No	No	No	Yes
Rename user	No	No	No	Yes	No
View Delete History	No	No	Yes	No	No
Import	No	No	Yes	No	No
Import upload	No	No	Yes	No	No
Minor Edit	No	Yes	No	No	No
Auto Confirm	No	No	Yes	No	Yes

This list is default for MediaWiki version 1.9.3. By the time this book is published, a new version might have some more access features for different access types. It is always mandatory to look at the `DefaultSettings.php` file for different user accesses allowed in the site.

Changing User Rights

We have seen so far that one can create an account, as well as read and edit articles without creating an account. Sometime this default option gives us security concerns, as a lot of users can access the system without registering to the site. It can prompt vandalism in the site. In order to prevent such activities, many wiki sites require users to register first if they want to access the system. We can also do this for our wiki site by editing the default settings in the DefaultSettings.php file. We can allow new access types to user groups as well as reduce access rights for particular users.

In order to change the default configuration for user rights, just copy the following code section from DefaultSettings.php file and paste it into localsettings.php.

```
$wgGroupPermissions = array();

$wgGroupPermissions['*'     ]['createaccount']   = true;
$wgGroupPermissions['*'     ]['read']            = true;
$wgGroupPermissions['*'     ]['edit']            = true;
$wgGroupPermissions['user'  ]['move']            = true;
$wgGroupPermissions['user'  ]['read']            = true;
$wgGroupPermissions['user'  ]['edit']            = true;
$wgGroupPermissions['user'  ]['upload']          = true;

$wgGroupPermissions['bot'   ]['bot']             = true;

$wgGroupPermissions['sysop']['block']            = true;
$wgGroupPermissions['sysop']['createaccount']    = true;
$wgGroupPermissions['sysop']['delete']           = true;
$wgGroupPermissions['sysop']['editinterface']    = true;
$wgGroupPermissions['sysop']['import']           = true;
$wgGroupPermissions['sysop']['importupload']     = true;
$wgGroupPermissions['sysop']['move']             = true;
$wgGroupPermissions['sysop']['patrol']           = true;
$wgGroupPermissions['sysop']['protect']          = true;
$wgGroupPermissions['sysop']['rollback']         = true;
$wgGroupPermissions['sysop']['upload']           = true;

$wgGroupPermissions['bureaucrat']['userrights']  = true;
$wgGroupPermissions['bureaucrat']['renameuser']  = true;
```

In the code section, we can see that all general user permissions are stored in an array. The first column of the array indicates the user type and the second column indicates access type. If you are not familiar with PHP, do not panic. We are not going to show complex operations using a PHP array; we will just explore the code section to make a meaningful one for us.

The first line creates an array. We will be storing different value in this array.

```
$wgGroupPermissions = array();
```

The second line indicates that all users, including anonymous users, can create an account. The symbol * stands for all uses including anonymous or unregistered users. If we set the second line to be false, then no new user can register on our site. Look at the following example:

```
$wgGroupPermissions['*'    ]['createaccount']    = False;
```

This will block users from creating new accounts from the site. You can change this to false if you want to configure your site to be a restricted area where only few people or groups of selected people can join.

If you want to turn off the edit option, then do the following:

```
$wgGroupPermissions['*'    ]['edit']              = False;
```

If we set account creation and edit options to be false, then no one can edit articles in the site and no new user can be created.

Let us now disable the create-new-page option. So users cannot create any new page! What are we trying to do here? Look at the features closely. Users can only leave their comment on talk pages and can do nothing else. Sysop can do everything. If there is just a single sysop, then the wiki becomes a blog. Isn't it amazing? We can use the wiki as a blog by just resetting few variables. Can we turn a wiki site to a forum? The answer is yes. Just turn on the new-page-creation option and turn off the edit option. User can then create new pages (similar to a forum post), and can leave comments on talk pages (equivalent to forum reply).

This way we can set different configuration options according to our need. We can also create new user groups on our wiki site if it is required. Just append to the $wgGroupPermissions array with our new user type and access permissions. Let's say we want to create a new user group named Ghost. Also, we want to give the new group privileges to read, delete, and upload. The code section that we have to append for this is:

```
$wgGroupPermissions['Ghost']['delete'] = true;
$wgGroupPermissions['Ghost']['read'] = true;
$wgGroupPermissions['Ghost']['upload'] = true;
```

Save the page, and we are done. Isn't it straightforward? Now let's see how we can assign a particular user to a group.

Granting Permissions to Users

You can grant permission to any existing user to any existing group by changing the user's group name. But in order to grant rights you must have an account of bureaucrat or sysop type. During installation, we created the sysop account, so we can use that account information to login as a sysop and grant an existing user a particular right. You have to perform the following steps in order to grant rights to users:

1. Log in as a sysop or a bureaucrat. It is the same login that we have created during the installation process.

2. Click the **Special pages** link from the toolbox.

3. In the special pages list, there are few restricted pages, listed at the bottom of the page. The last link is the **User rights management** link. Click the link to access the page.

4. When you are on the **User rights management** page, provide an existing user name in the user name input box and click the **Edit User Groups** button. You will see something similar to the following image.

5. This is a window with current access groups as well as available access groups for the particular user. You can choose more than one of the available groups to be assigned for the user. In order to choose more than one group from the available list, press the *Ctrl* key on the keyboard and select the desired group.

6. Save the page by clicking the **Save User Groups** button. The user rights have been granted for the user ghosthunter. If ghosthunter is logged in during this process, then the rights will be effective when he or she logs in the next time.

7. If you want to remove particular rights for a user, then select that option from the **Member of** list and save the page. The user will be removed from the selected rights group.

Blocking Users

Sometimes it is inevitable that users will do something silly or harm to your site. They might try to delete paragraphs from articles or change pages randomly without reason. This kind of activity can be counted as vandalism. If you want to block these users from accessing your site, you can do that with a special page named **Block user**. You can block by specifying either a particular user name or an IP. Here are the steps to block a user or IP address:

1. Log in as a sysop or a bureaucrat. It is the same login we have created during the installation process.

2. Go to the special page section.

3. In the special page list, there are few restricted pages listed in the bottom part of the page. There is a link named **Block user**. Click the link to access the following page:

4. Enter the **IP Address** or the **username** you want to block.

5. Choose an expiry time after which that particular user or IP address can not access the system.

   You can enter your desired time to expire the user access if the option is not available in expiry list.

6. Put a reason why the user or IP address has been blocked so that a bureaucrat or another sysop knows the reason for blocking.

7. You can also block anonymous users from a particular IP and allow access to registered users from the same IP by checking the first checkbox. If you check the second checkbox, then no user can register from the given IP address. If you check the last checkbox, then you can stop the user from editing anything from the IP address he or she last used, and the subsequent addresses from which he or she might try to edit.

8. Save the page by clicking **Block this user** button.

Protecting a Page

Sometimes it is necessary to protect a page against vandalism or other unwanted edits. First of all, visit the page in question and click the **protect** tab in the article tab section. You will be presented with one of two boxes, depending on the version of MediaWiki your wiki is running. Follow the steps as stated here:

1. Enter the reason for protecting the page in the text box.

2. If you want to protect the page only from being moved, then check the box below, which indicates **protect from moves only**.

3. Now click the **confirm** button to protect the page.

4. To *unprotect* a page, click the **unprotect** tab. This will bring up the same page as above, only this time without the move checkbox. A reason for unprotecting should be given in the unprotect page and saved.

MediaWiki namespace: Only sysops can edit pages in the protected MediaWiki namespace.

Editing: To edit a previously protected page as an administrator, just click the **edit** tab. The only difference now is that there is a warning at the top of the page indicating that the page has been protected, but it can be edited like any other non-protected page.

Images: Protecting an image is mostly the same as protecting a page. When the **protect** tab is clicked on the image description page, both the page and the image are protected. The image description page will be protected. Once this is done, non-sysops will not be able to revert the image to an earlier version, or upload a new version over it.

Deleting a Page

Administrators can delete pages and their history, and can view and restore deleted pages and their history. They can also delete images, but this is irreversible—once an image is deleted, it cannot be restored. So before deleting any page or image, we have to be careful about the action.

To *delete* a page, click the **delete** link on the page that is to be deleted. This will bring up a new page asking for a confirmation that the page should be deleted, as well as an explanation for the deletion. A message should be typed into the input box to explain the deletion to other users. After the page has been deleted, any existing talk page for that page should be deleted as well. Any links that point to the deleted page should be removed or corrected.

Allowing File Uploads

We know how to upload a file. We have already uploaded files, especially image-type files. We can also upload other file types by modifying our configuration. The allowed file type list is available under `DefaultSettings.php` file. In order to change this configuration, we have to copy the following line from `DefaultSettings.php` and paste it into the `localsettings.php` file:

```
$wgFileExtensions = array( 'png', 'gif', 'jpg', 'jpeg' );
```

Now if we want to allow uploading `.zip`, `.pdf`, `.doc`, and other types of files, then we have to add those extensions to the end of the array separated by comma. Such as:

```
$wgFileExtensions = array( 'png', 'gif', 'jpg', 'jpeg', 'zip' ,
                           'pdf' , 'doc', 'ppt', 'xls');
```

Before making the changes in the `localsettings.php` file, we have to make sure that we have checked both the file black list and mime-type black list variables (shown in the code that follows) in `DefaultSettings.php`. These two variables contain all the blocked file types in order to make the system safe. By default these are file types those are not allowed for upload, and it's recommended that they're not allowed by administrator.

```
/** Files with these extensions will never be allowed as uploads. */
$wgFileBlacklist = array(
    # HTML may contain cookie-stealing JavaScript and web bugs
    'html', 'htm', 'js', 'jsb',
    # PHP scripts may execute arbitrary code on the server
    'php', 'phtml', 'php3', 'php4', 'phps',
    # Other types that may be interpreted by some servers
    'shtml', 'jhtml', 'pl', 'py', 'cgi',
```

```
    # May contain harmful executables for Windows victims
    'exe', 'scr', 'dll', 'msi', 'vbs', 'bat', 'com', 'pif',
                                    'cmd', 'vxd', 'cpl' );

/** Files with these mime types will never be allowed as uploads
 * if $wgVerifyMimeType is enabled.
 */
$wgMimeTypeBlacklist= array(
    # HTML may contain cookie-stealing JavaScript and web bugs
    'text/html', 'text/javascript', 'text/x-javascript',
    'application/x-shellscript',
    # PHP scripts may execute arbitrary code on the server
    'application/x-php', 'text/x-php',
    # Other types that may be interpreted by some servers
    'text/x-python', 'text/x-perl', 'text/x-bash', 'text/x-sh',
                                        'text/x-csh',
    # Windows metafile, client-side vulnerability on some systems
    'application/x-msmetafile'
);
```

We can also check the file type on upload. We can use `$wgCheckFileExtensions` to determine whether file extensions are checked on upload. `$wgStrictFileExtensions` can be used to set strict file types checking. We can define the maximum size for file upload by defining the `$wgUploadSizeWarning` variable in the `localsettings.php` file. This will generate a warning message if the file size is more than the warning level.

Security Checklist

This is the most important task of an administrator. The administrator is the person who will make sure the site is secure from different types of attacks and vulnerability. As a system admin, you have to perform some checks on regular basis. It is better if you make a checklist of all the required actions and go through them at least once a week (or more frequently if required). Here are the checks that you must perform:

Stay Up to Date

It is always important to stay up to date regarding the installed software. We are not installing a final product. We have to remember that frequently we have a version release for MediaWiki. Each version contains a release note. Go through the release note and see if any vulnerability has been fixed. Even if it does not contain any security update, it is always better to update the server software. It is not just MediaWiki that needs to be updated—we have to update PHP, MySQL and other installed software in our web server as well. In order to get messages from MediaWiki about updates and news, you can subscribe to the following site for email notifications: `http://mail.wikipedia.org/mailman/listinfo/mediawiki-announce`.

PHP Recommendations

If you are using a shared host, then you might not have access to the PHP setup file. However, if you are running a dedicated server or your local server at home or in your office, you can set up the PHP configuration file yourself. The file name is `PHP.ini`. It is located under `c:\windows\php.ini` on Windows, and under `/etc/php.ini` in a Linux environment. Here are my recommendations:

- Disable `register_globals`:

  Many PHP security attacks are based on injection of global variable values, and so, making sure it's off can make many potential vulnerabilities toothless. MediaWiki should be safe even if this is on; turning this off is a precaution against the possibility of unknown vulnerabilities.

- Unless you require it specifically, disable `allow_url_fopen`:

  Remote PHP code execution vulnerabilities may depend on being able to inject a URL into `include()` or `require()`. If you don't require the use of remote file loading, turning this off can prevent attacks of this kind on vulnerable code.

- Disable `session.use_trans_sid`:

  If this is on, session IDs may be added to URLs sometimes if cookies aren't doing their thing. This can leak login session data to third-party sites through referrer data or cut and paste of links. You should always turn this off if it's on.

MySQL Recommendations

In general, you should keep access to your MySQL database to a minimum. If it will only be used from the single machine it's running on, consider disabling networking support. If it will be used over a network with a limited number of client machines, consider setting the IP firewall rules to accept access to TCP port 3306 for MySQL only from those machines or only from your local subnet, and reject all accesses from the larger Internet. This can help prevent accidentally opening access to your server due to some unknown flaw in MySQL, a mistakenly set overbroad GRANT, or a leaked password.

If you create a new MySQL user for MediaWiki through MediaWiki's installer, somewhat liberal access is granted to it to ensure that it will work from a second server as well as a local one. You might consider manually narrowing this or establishing the user account yourself with custom permissions from just the places you need.

Creating Interwiki Links

As the name suggests an interwiki link is link between two different wikis. We have already learned about the usage of interwiki links. Now we will learn how to add new interwiki links by following the steps given below:

1. Log in to your MySQL server using phpMyAdmin (as most of the hosted servers use this as a third-party tool).

2. Select the installed database from the **database** list on the left navigation panel.

3. Click on the **interwiki** table to load the table. You will see the current list of interwiki links that are defined.

4. Click on the **Insert** tab from the top-navigation bar of the page and you will be directed to the insert page for new interwiki links.

5. Put your new prefix in the box labeled with **iw_prefix** and the URL of the prefix at **iw_url**. If the target wiki is local then set the **iw_local** to be **1**. You can enter a URL to be `http://en.wikipedia.org/wiki/` or `http://en.wikipedia.org/wiki/$1`. Here $1 will be replaced by the target name followed by the prefix in the declaration, which we will see in a short while.

6. After that click on the **Go** button to insert the record and you can continue until you are done with your interwiki list.

Server: **localhost** ▸ Database: **haunted** ▸ Table: **interwiki**

| | Structure | Browse | SQL | Search | Insert | Export | Operations | Empty | Drop |

InnoDB free: 7168 kB

Field	Type	Function	Null	Value
iw_prefix	char(32)			
iw_url	char(127)			
iw_local	tinyint(1)			0
iw_trans	tinyint(1)			0

☑ Ignore

Field	Type	Function	Null	Value
iw_prefix	char(32)			
iw_url	char(127)			
iw_local	tinyint(1)			0
iw_trans	tinyint(1)			0

Insert as a new row -- **And** --
⦿ Go back to previous page
Or
○ Insert another new row

[Go] [Reset]

Say for example you want to create a new interwiki link for Wikipedia and for that you enter WikiPedia in the **iw_prefix** row, http://en.wikipedia.org/wiki/$1 in the **iw_url**, and click **Go** button. It will create the new interwiki link and you can use the link as the following code:

```
[[:iw_prefix:target name]]
```

Here iw_prefix is the interwiki prefix name and target name is the link we want to visit. So as a result, the code [[:WikiPedia:Haunted]], will take us to the http://en.wikipedia.org/wiki/Haunted page.

Summary

In this chapter we have learned things like configuring MediaWiki installation to work better, and we have seen a security checklist, and administrator activities to make our site better. This is just start of the administration part. We have to know more about administrative tasks such as customizing different options and also extending our installation to be more powerful, and to make the site more feature-rich. We'll see these things along with some other interesting hacks in the next chapter, where we will talk about customizing MediaWiki.

8
Customizing MediaWiki

In the last chapter, we focused on administrating different aspects of MediaWiki. However, we have not yet discussed how to change things according to our preferences i.e. customization. So far we have seen how to change the look, using the visible control from the application; a few things, however, need us to code, which means we need to add or change things *inside* the files to customize the application to what we want. We have a lot of options for customizing the application. We can add, remove, and modify features according to our need. We can change skins, add new functionalities, modify existing features, etc., with our knowledge of PHP. In this chapter, we will basically learn about modifying existing features. In the next chapter, we will learn how to add new functionality in our application.

What We Can Customize

The most important question we need to ask is what can be customized in MediaWiki? Before going into detail, see the image overleaf. We have changed the look of our wiki site completely. Want to know how we can do such things? Well, we can do much of this type of "magic" by **customizing** MediaWiki; keep reading the chapter, and by its end, you will find that you know a lot of useful things. As you can see in the following example, you can customize layouts, skins, and the navigation bar. All of these customizations and many more will be covered in this chapter. So fasten your seat belt for a technical and joyful ride.

In this chapter we will dig into the MediaWiki code base. So you must have some knowledge of PHP as well as CSS, because we will explore lots of code sections in this chapter — something that has not been done in this book so far.

We can divide our customization decisions into two parts:

- Appearance
- Page layout

On the appearance front, we can change the background color and image, the font color, font type, graphics, buttons, logo, etc. As far as the page layout is concerned, we can rearrange our content blocks and place them in different positions according to our choice. The previous image is a concrete example of changing the appearance of a wiki site by changing the logo, background image, and other properties. In this chapter, we will first learn how to customize our existing MediaWiki skins and, at the end of the chapter, we will focus more on creating a new skin with a new layout from scratch.

Knowing the File Structure

MediaWiki layout largely depends on which skin you are using. We have seen in the user preference setting how to choose a skin from the available skins in MediaWiki. By default, the monobook skin is chosen. So in this book we will mostly talk about the monobook skin and how to modify the existing skin for layout changes. We are talking about skins; so let's understand what skins really are.

A skin is a PHP class that contains all the necessary functions to generate HTML output for each wiki page that will be shown in our browser. What really happens is that each available skin in MediaWiki is a different class that inherits the Skin class and implements each of the necessary functions to draw the page. In the MediaWiki installation directory, we have a folder named `skins`. If you browse the folder, you will see a few PHP files, which are the skin files, and a few folders with the same names as the PHP files. These folders contain Cascading Style Sheet (CSS) files for each skin. Here is a view of the default MediaWiki directory:

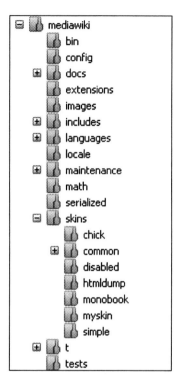

 Skin files vary over different versions of MediaWiki. So skins become obsolete over time. A skin in version 1.3 might not exist in version 1.4, and so on.

The core skin class and other associated classes are inside the `includes` folder of the MediaWiki installation directory. The names of those classes are:

- `Skin.php`
- `SkinTemplate.php`

The `SkinTemplate` class inherits the `Skin` class. These are the files responsible for what we see on screen. These classes return different bits of HTML code. However, what is it that holds things together? Which class actually decides the layout of the page on screen? Well, *none* of these classes is used for that! Earlier, we talked about the `skins` folder, and all the skin definitions reside in this folder. The example we have shown in the first image of this chapter, used the monobook skin. So if you open the `MonoBook.php` file, you will see many division tags (`<div>`) have been used to hold the pieces together to show the page's structure. The content returned from skin classes is shown properly using the HTML structure in the appropriate skin file. You must remember that if you want to change the layout, then you have to change the specific skin file in the `skins` folder, not the `Skin.php` file in the `includes` folder. For example if you want to change the layout for `MonoBook` skin then you have to change the `MonoBook.php` file inside the `skins` folder and the `Skin.php` file should not be changed. We will learn about skins later on in this chapter. If you want to change the page content, then you can change the `Skin.php` and other files, which you will discover as the chapter progresses.

Understanding the Skin File

We will now analyze our default skin file, `MonoBook.php`. Let's open the `MonoBook.php` file in the `skins` directory and examine it. Since the file is big, we will only see a small part of it to get an understanding of the structure. The first part of the skin file contains the block of PHP code where the `MonoBook` skin class is created by extending the existing `SkinTemplate` and `QuickTemplate` classes. For now, we will not try to understand the meaning of these code blocks, as we will be doing it later in the chapter, when we write our own skin file. The main function that describes the layout and contents of the skin is the `execute` function under the `MonoBookTemplate` class. The code block is as follows:

```
class MonoBookTemplate extends QuickTemplate
{
  /**
   * Template filter callback for MonoBook skin.
   * Takes an associative array of data set from a SkinTemplate-based
   * class, and a wrapper for MediaWiki's localization database, and
   * outputs a formatted page.
   *
   * @access private
   */
  function execute() {
    // Suppress warnings to prevent notices about missing indexes in
    // $this->data
    wfSuppressWarnings();
?>
```

After the above code block, we have an XHTML code section up to the end of the `MonoBook.php` file. The XHTML page template consists of a number of div sections. Each div is identified by either or both an `id` and `class` attribute in the `<div>` tag. The stylesheet then controls *how* each div block is drawn, and *where* on the page it is positioned.

Take a look at the following code snippet of the `monobook.php` file:

```php
<div class="portlet" id="p-personal">
  <h5><?php $this->msg('personaltools') ?></h5>
  <div class="pBody">
    <ul>
    <?php foreach($this->data['personal_urls'] as $key => $item) {
      ?><li id="pt-<?php echo htmlspecialchars($key) ?>"><a
                                                     href="<?php
      echo htmlspecialchars($item['href']) ?>"<?php
      if(!empty($item['class'])) { ?> class="<?php
      echo htmlspecialchars($item['class']) ?>"<?php } ?>><?php
      echo htmlspecialchars($item['text']) ?></a></li>
    <?php } ?>
    </ul>
  </div>
</div>
<div class="portlet" id="p-logo">
  <a style="background-image: url(<?php $this->text('logopath') ?>);"
                                  <?php
  ?> href="<?php echo htmlspecialchars($this->
                        data['nav_urls']['mainpage']['href'])?>"
  <?php title="<?php $this->msg('mainpage') ?>"></a>
</div>
```

As you can see in the code section, there is a division with ID `p-personal` and class `portlet`. These `<div>` tags work as individual blocks and together they build the layout of the page. If you examine the full code section, you will find that a lot of such `<div>` have been used, and corresponding stylesheets have been declared in the folders named according to the skin names. So for the monobook skin, we have a folder named `monobook`, and the CSS file is `main.css`, which defines the style rules for the page. The `portlet` class, which we have seen in the code snippet, defines the basic style of the div blocks not part of the main content area. Each block is furnished with the style defined for it in the stylesheet that is referred to by the `div` ID or class.

The main page section is a block with the ID `column-content`, which contains the block with the ID `content`. The `content` block contains the main content heading with the `firstHeading` class and the `bodyContent` block, which contains a subheading identifying the MediaWiki site name, the `contentSub` block, the actual page contents, and a `visualClear` block. Let's explore a few important identifiers in the `main.css` file for the monobook skin.

- `column-content` is used to define the overall space within the margins of which the content exists.
- `content` is the white background, thin bordered box that contains the content for the main page.

- `firstHeading` is the class of the `heading` tag at the top of every page.
- `bodyContent` actually contains the main page content within the content box.
- `contentSub` defines the style of text that indicates the name of the wiki immediately underneath the main heading, but above the body text.

The portlets section is a block with the ID `column-one`, containing portlet blocks with the IDs `p-cactions`, `p-personal`, `p-logo`, `p-nav`, `p-search`, and `p-tb`. At the bottom of the page is a block with the ID `footer`, containing the `f-poweredbyico` and `f-list` blocks. The `portlet.css` class is the style used by all the div blocks around the main content. Here are the identified blocks using that class:

article	discussion	edit	history	protect	delete	move	watch

- `p-cactions` is the ID for the list of tabs above the main content.

Admin   my talk   my preferences   my watchlist   my contributions   log out

- `p-personal` is the ID for the list of links that include the login or logout page at the top of the page.

Set $wgLogo to the URL path to your own logo image.

- `p-logo` is the ID for the block that contains the logo (on the top left).

navigation
- Main Page
- Community portal
- Current events
- Recent changes
- Random page
- Help
- Donations

- p-nav is the ID for the block that contains the navigation links on the left of the page.

- p-search is the block that contains the search buttons.

- p-tb is the block that contains the toolbox links.

The footer at the bottom of the page includes blocks with the following IDs:

- footer is the block that contains the overall footer.

- f-list is the list for all additional links in the footer section except the copyright and powered-by icon.

We now know about the layout and style properties for skins. We will explore changing the layout and then modifying the CSS to change the look of the site to the one we have shown in the example.

Customizing the Layout

We will now show you how to change the layout. We have many options with regards to what can be changed, but in this section we will show you how to change the logo and the page footer, as well as how to move sections to change the layout of your site.

Changing the Logo

So far in the book, we have used the default logo that was set during the installation process. Now it is high time to change it to our own. In order to change our logo, we have to take the following steps:

1. Put the desired image in the `image` folder of your web server.

2. Add the following two lines at the end of the `LocalSettings.php` file, but before the `?>` mark:

   ```
   $wgStylePath    =   "$wgScriptPath/skins";
   $wgLogo         =   "$wgStylePath/common/images/hauntedlogo.jpg";
   ```

3. Put the exact location of the image and name of the image file in the `$wgLogo` variable. In this code we have shown the setup for this book's example.

4. Save the file and reload the page in your browser; you will see the new logo on the pages.

Changing the Footer

We have changed our logo settings in the last paragraph by simply substituting the logo variable's value. In this example, we will see how we can remove unwanted content from our skin. Let us start with a simple example—removing a part of the footer. Here is the default footer shown in the monobook style:

As you can see, there is some information shown in the footer section, such as the time of the last edit, total number of times the article has been viewed, about us, and disclaimers. Suppose you want to remove the last edit section from the footer. In order to change that, we have to analyze the footer code section of the PHP file. The footer section for the previous screenshot is as follows:

```php
<div id="footer">
<?php
    if($this->data['poweredbyico']) { ?>
        <div id="f-poweredbyico">
                        <?php $this->html('poweredbyico') ?></div>
```

```php
<?php    }
    if($this->data['copyrightico']) { ?><div id=
        "f-copyrightico"><?php $this->html('copyrightico') ?></div>
<?php    }

    // Generate additional footer links
?>
    <ul id="f-list">
<?php
    $footerlinks = array(
        'lastmod', 'viewcount', 'numberofwatchingusers', 'credits',
            'copyright', 'privacy', 'about', 'disclaimer', 'tagline',
    );
    foreach( $footerlinks as $aLink ) {
        if( isset( $this->data[$aLink] ) && $this->data[$aLink] ) {
?>        <li id="<?php echo$aLink?>"><?php $this->html($aLink) ?></li>
<?php        }
    }
?>
    </ul>
</div>
```

As you can see, the `$footerlinks` array contains the additional footer options to show, including the last modification time. If we remove that option from the array, then it won't be shown as part of the footer anymore. So if we remove the option, the code will look like:

```php
$footerlinks = array(
    'viewcount', 'numberofwatchingusers', 'credits', 'copyright',
    'privacy', 'about', 'disclaimer', 'tagline',
);
```

After changing the code, we have to save the page. Now refresh the browser, and you can see the changes in the footer section:

This page has been accessed 132 times.	Privacy policy	About Haunted	Disclaimers	

 Sometimes the changes might not be visible in the browser after saving and reloading the file. In such cases, you need to clear the browser cache and reload the page, or press *Ctrl+R* or *F5* to reload the page from the server, and then you will see the changed page.

We have just seen that we can remove any unwanted part from the footer section. Similarly, we can add content to the footer section if required.

Moving Sections

So far the examples were straightforward and easy to understand. Let's try another one, which is little bit more challenging — we are going to move a complete section from its original place. This part is tricky because we have to move the complete code section and place it in our desired location while ensuring that there is no overlapping with any other section. If the section is not moved properly, then it might break the page layout. So here is the task we are going to perform. We always see the search box between the navigation bar and the toolbox. Why don't we move the search bar above the navigation bar or just below the toolbar? The search box's code section can be found in the MonoBook.php file. Look for the following code section:

```
<div id="p-search" class="portlet">
    <h5><label for="searchInput"><?php $this->msg('search')
                                    ?></label></h5>
    <div id="searchBody" class="pBody">
      <form action="<?php $this->text('searchaction')
                                    ?>" id="searchform"><div>
        <input id="searchInput" name="search" type="text" <?php
          if($this->haveMsg('accesskey-search')) {
            ?>accesskey="<?php $this->msg('accesskey-search') ?>"<?php }
          if( isset( $this->data['search'] ) ) {
            ?> value="<?php $this->text('search') ?>"<?php } ?> />
        <input type='submit' name="go" class="searchButton"
            id="searchGoButton"  value="<?php
            $this->msg('searcharticle') ?>" /> 
        <input type='submit' name="fulltext" class="searchButton"
            id="mw-searchButton" value="<?php
            $this->msg('searchbutton') ?>" />
      </div></form>
    </div>
  </div>
```

This code section is responsible for the search option on the page. If you want to move the search section to the bottom of the left column, then you have to find the following code section in the page:

```php
<?php
    if ( $this->data['language_urls'] ) { ?>
  <div id="p-lang" class="portlet">
    <h5><?php $this->msg('otherlanguages') ?></h5>
    <div class="pBody">
      <ul>
<?php    foreach($this->data['language_urls'] as $langlink) { ?>
        <li class="<?php echo htmlspecialchars($langlink['class'])
        ?>"><?php
        ?><a href="<?php echo htmlspecialchars($langlink['href'])
        ?>"><?php echo $langlink['text'] ?></a></li>
<?php    } ?>
      </ul>
    </div>
  </div>
<?php  } ?>
</div><!-- end of the left (by default at least) column -->
```

The code says it all—especially the comment at the end of the code section. So in order to show the search section at the bottom of the left column, we have to cut and paste the search portion just above the last </div> shown in the code you just saw, save it, review it in the browser, and we are done! This is just a piece of cake. We will need to make this kind of modification every now and then. The reason we have been doing this simple modification is to get the hang of making changes easily. For a novice, these things might sound interesting, but for expert, these things may not be significant. If you want to alter the view of the pages, then another way of doing things is changing the PHP files, which will be discussed later in this chapter.

Customizing the Skin Using CSS

We have seen that things are done using CSS in the monobook file. Every HTML element has an ID and class defined, and the corresponding style is defined in the main.css file. So far in this book, we have seen the default skin for MediaWiki. Now, do you remember the well-designed MediaWiki site that we saw at the start of this chapter? We are going to follow a step-by-step procedure to produce that same look. Our main focus will be on the main.css file. We will explore how small changes in the CSS file can revamp the look of the existing design. First let's make a to-do list for the changes:

1. Change the background image.
2. Change the text color for the site.

Changing the Background Image

MediaWiki uses its default background image and color for the monobook skin. However, we can change the background image and color anytime we want. To change the background color, we go inside the `main.css` file. Inside the `main.css` file, we have a class defined for the `body` tag. The default rule for the `body` tag is as follows:

```
body {
    font: x-small sans-serif;
    background: #f9f9f9 url(headbg.jpg) 0 0 no-repeat;
    color: black;
    margin: 0;
    padding: 0;
}
```

As you can see, the body color defined here is close to gray, and the font color is black. Also, the body uses one header image at the top of every page. You can also view the header image just above the **Article** tab. We want to change everything, starting with the background color, the font, and the background image. As our aim is to make changes reflecting the example style, first we need to change the background color to dark gray, and also change the background image. The background image must be placed inside the appropriate skin folder. Here is the change that has to be made to the `background` property of the `body` rule:

```
background: #EDEDED url(bg_b.gif) 0 0 repeat-x;
```

Save the CSS file and reload the page in the browser. When you load the page, you will see the following screen:

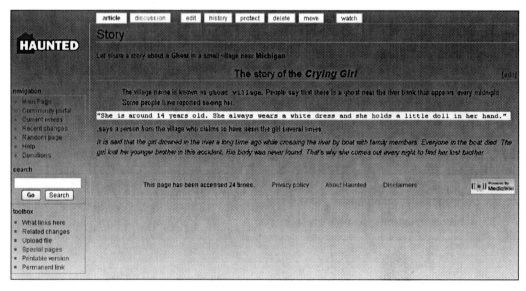

Note: If you do no see your desired result on the screen after making all required changes. Then clear your browser cache and reload the page again.

It looks like we are almost there, but it's a case of "so near, and yet so far". You can see the white blocks within the screen, where we do not see the background image of the page. We could change the blocks' background color, but that will not solve our problem. We need to do something that will make the blocks *transparent*! How and where do we make a change for such an effect?

The left-side navigation and toolbox area style is defined by the pBody class in the main.css file. The default definition of the class is as follows:

```
.pBody {
    font-size: 95%;
    background-color: white;
    color: black;
    border-collapse: collapse;
    border: 1px solid #aaa;
    padding: 0 .8em .3em .5em;
}
```

As of now, the background is defined to be white. Replace the line with the background-color property with the following one:

```
background: transparent;
```

For the main content section, we have the content selector defined in CSS. Here we have to change the background to be transparent as has been done with the pBody class.

```
#content {
            background: transparent;
            color: black;
            border: 1px solid #aaa;
            border-right: none;
            line-height: 1.5em;
}
```

The last change we need to make involves making the footer section transparent. The footer section would then look as follows:

```
#footer {
            background: transparent;
            border-top: 1px solid #fabd23;
            border-bottom: 1px solid #fabd23;
            margin: .6em 0 1em 0;
            padding: .4em 0 1.2em 0;
```

```
text-align: center;
font-size: 90%;
}
```

Save the `main.css` file with the changes, and reload the page in your browser. Here's what you should see:

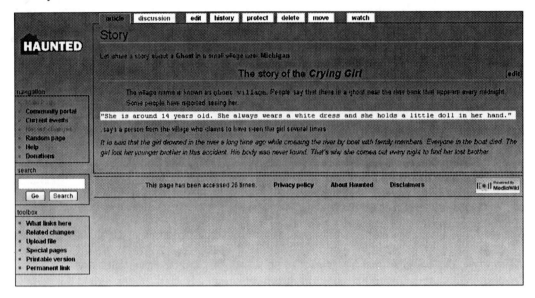

Much better! However, the text for the top navigation seems to have blended in with the background; we can hardly see the text at the top of the page! So we have another job left, which is to change the text color to black so as to create a nice contrast on the page. We will see the corresponding CSS entries and the required changes.

For simplicity, changes will be shown one after another. To make changes to the CSS, go to the declaration and replace the relevant lines with the required change.

The rule for general hyperlinks is defined as follows (this rule is used in the toolbox and navigation panel in general):

```
a {
    text-decoration: none;
    color: #002bb8;
    background: none;
}

a:visited {
        color: #5a3696;
}
a:active {
        color: #faa700;
}
```

To change the color of the links and to make them bold to create a stronger presence on the screen, replace the previous code with the following:

```
a {
    text-decoration: none;
    color: #000000;
    background: none;
    font-weight: bold;
}
a:visited {
            color: #C36200;
}
a:active {
            color: #000000;
            font-weight: bold;
}
```

The same needs to be done for the top links shown at the top-right corner, tabs on the main page, and the selected tab on a page. Change the font color to black, and the tab to be same as the background color. For this, you need to change the declarations as follows:

```
/* for top links */

#p-personal li a
{
   text-decoration: none;
   color: #000000;
   padding-bottom: .2em;
   background: none;
}

/* for tab shown on main content */

#p-cactions li a
{
   background-color: #fbfbfb;
   color: #000000;
   border: none;
   padding: 0 .8em .3em;
   position: relative;
   z-index: 0;
   margin: 0;
   text-decoration: none;
}

#p-cactions li.selected a
{
   z-index: 3;
```

```
        padding: 0 1em .2em!important;
        background-color: #3C7FAF;
}
```

We have already seen the content CSS property defined to make the background transparent. We need to change the color property there to make the font color black and also change the border of the blocks to black. The same code will apply there. After changing all the required definition, save the `main.css` file and reload the page in your browser. You will see a screen similar to this one:

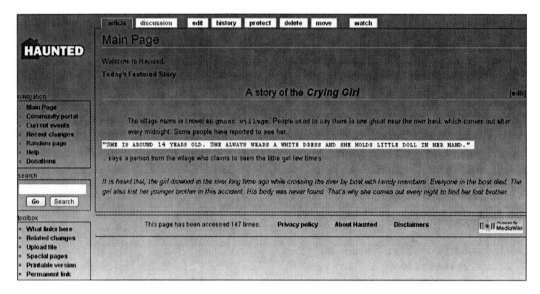

This is exactly what we have been looking for, and we have created it by making a few CSS modifications. This is the way we have to change the look of the site. It is not only limited to changing the color and transparency, but we can also change the size of the blocks such as expanding the logo block to incorporate logo and advertisement, change the font type, the orientation of the page by shifting `<div>`s, and so on. So, to sum up the discussion of this section, we can conclude that CSS is an important component to be used when designing nice-looking layouts and visuals. This is, however, not where customization ends. You can customize the site by changing the PHP files too, which is what we will learn in the next section.

Customizing Using Core Files

In the last section, we saw that we can customize our layout by using CSS and changing the tags. In this section, we will explore customization by editing the core PHP files. So what can we customize in PHP that we cannot with CSS? What about showing some links or contents to users after login? Can we hide those things using CSS? The answer is "No". We can move things around or remove them, but cannot put any conditions in CSS to set content as visible or invisible. For this kind of customization, we need PHP to help us out. We will now see such customization applied in our wiki.

In some cases, you might need to disable the registration option for new users on the site. You might want to restrict automatic user registration and only want registrations to be performed by the administrator. This task is not that easy, as there is a link labeled **Log in/create account** on every page of your wiki. Anyone can use this link to create an account, and the only way to restrict this is by changing the PHP file associated with it. This can be done in two ways:

- Changing the core PHP file
- Changing the MonoBook.php file

We will cover both methods, but first let's explore the easier way.

Disabling Registrations Using the Skin File

In this method, we will change the default skin file of the wiki to disable the registration link. As our default skin is monobook, we will modify the MonoBook.php file. This method is easier because it requires less time to make the change and understand the code than the other one. Although this method is easier, it requires making the same change on all skins where this link is available, whereas if we change the core PHP file, changes to skins won't be required. In the MonoBook.php file, search for the following section:

```php
<?php foreach($this->data['personal_urls'] as $key => $item) {
        ?><li id="pt-<?php echo htmlspecialchars($key) ?>"><a
href="<?php
        echo htmlspecialchars($item['href']) ?>"<?php
        if(!empty($item['class'])) { ?> class="<?php
        echo htmlspecialchars($item['class']) ?>"<?php } ?>><?php
        echo htmlspecialchars($item['text']) ?></a></li><?php
    } ?>
```

This code section is responsible for showing personal URLs at the top-right corner of every page. It can be a **login** link, a **create account** link, your IP address, etc. You would have to change this code block to not show the **create account** option. This is what the changed code block should look like:

```php
<?php foreach($this->data['personal_urls'] as $key => $item) {
        if ($key != 'login') {
        ?><li id="pt-<?php echo htmlspecialchars($key) ?>"><a
href="<?php
        echo htmlspecialchars($item['href']) ?>"<?php
        if(!empty($item['class'])) { ?> class="<?php
        echo htmlspecialchars($item['class']) ?>"<?php } ?>><?php
        echo htmlspecialchars($item['text']) ?></a></li><?php
        }
    } ?>
```

As you can see from the highlighted code section, we have simply added one extra condition after the `for each` loop. It's checking if the key is for login. If it is for login, then we will not show the links for it, but we will show other items in the personal URL section. You have to remember to put closing braces at the end of the code section as in the highlighted code. Save the page and clear your browser's cache before running the changed file. After running it, you will see that the top link is gone for users who have not logged in. Isn't it great?

> As MediaWiki is growing at a rapid pace, there are new versions released more often than you might think; so it might happen that you will see a code section that is different from what is described here. In order to avoid such confusion, it is always better to understand the code section and identify the code section that you want to change. Comments in the code section can be very helpful on this regard.

Disabling Registrations Using the Core PHP File

We have disabled registrations by changing the style file for each style, but we can also do this by changing the core file, `SkinTemplate.php`. There is a line where this array is populated, and we will have to change this section so that the array is not populated and hence not shown on the page. Now you might wonder how I know that I have to change the `SkinTemplate.php` file. The answer is very simple; search your code base for the keyword `personal_urls`, and you will see that only one core file is using this keyword, and that is the `SkinTemplate.php` file. But which content needs to be changed there? Recall that we just changed the login item to not be shown. So we have to search for the login option in the `SkinTemplate` file. If we search the file, we will get the following code section:

```
    } else {
            $personal_urls['login'] = array(
                'text' => wfMsg('userlogin'),
                'href' => $this->makeSpecialUrl('Userlogin',
                        'returnto=' . $this->thisurl )
            );
    }
```

This code is assigning the text and URLs to perform the new user's registration and login tasks. So what we can do is comment out the section so that no values are assigned, and we are actually done. However, people can still register using the special page, as the page exists in the special pages section. We can either block the new user registration from the LocalSettings.php file as we have seen in the previous chapter, or if we want to remove the link completely, we can edit the special page to not show the link. However, this will not allow anyone to log in either, and you would not want to make the site like that. It is thus always better to know what you are looking for before making any changes.

Now let's take a better example here. Suppose for logged-in users we want to show the toolbox area where the user can access the special pages and also upload files. For obvious reasons, we would want to hide the toolbox for unregistered or non-logged-in users. This can be done using the theme file (MonoBook.php). In this file, you need to find and modify the following the section, containing the code for the toolbox:

```
<div class="portlet" id="p-tb">
    <h5><?php $this->msg('toolbox') ?></h5>
```

Let's make it available for only logged-in users. We can do that by changing the code to:

```
<div class="portlet" id="p-tb">
  <?php if($this->data['loggedin']) { ?>
    <h5><?php $this->msg('toolbox') ?></h5>
```

As you can see, we have added one extra line that checks if the user is logged in. in order to make this code work, we have to close the braces as well. Just below the changes, you will find a code section as follows:

```
        </ul>
    </div>
</div>
```

We have to close the braces here to complete the change. Here is the changed code:

```
      </ul>
    </div>
  <?php } ?>
    </div>
```

Save the page and reload it in the browser. The toolbox will be gone. Wonderful, isn't it? These are some of the first hacking tricks that we have learned, and throughout the chapter, we will learn more of them.

Changing Default Skin for the Site

If you want to change the default skin for the site, then you have to modify the LocalSettings.php file. The changed skin for the site will then be loaded as the default skin for all the site visitors unless they have set a different skin in their preferences — once users log in, they will see their chosen skin if it is different from the default one. Here is the code section that has to be changed:

```
$wgDefaultSkin = 'monobook';
```

One thing you have to remember here is that the skin name you put here must exist in the skins directory. This skin name needs to be the same as defined inside your skin file. In the above example we have used default skin monobook. So if you open the MonoBook.php file you will see the following code section where we are defining the name of the skin to be monobook (in the highlighted code below):

```
class SkinMonoBook extends SkinTemplate {
  /** Using monobook. */
  function initPage( &$out ) {
    SkinTemplate::initPage( $out );
    $this->skinname  = 'monobook';
    $this->stylename = 'monobook';
    $this->template  = 'MonoBookTemplate';
  }
}
```

Disabling the Skin Choosing Option for Users

If you want to stick with one skin for the whole site, then it will be a good idea to turn off the skin choosing option from the user preference page. You can do this by commenting out the skin preference code section in the includes/SpecialPreferences.php file. Find the skin code block that looks like the following code:

```
# Skin
    #
    $wgOut->addHTML( "<fieldset>\n<legend>\n" . wfMsg('skin') .
                                             "</legend>\n" );
    $mptitle = Title::newMainPage();
    $previewtext = wfMsg('skinpreview');
    # Only show members of Skin::getSkinNames() rather than
    # $skinNames (skins is all skin names from Language.php)
    $validSkinNames = Skin::getSkinNames();
    # Sort by UI skin name. First though need to update
                                validSkinNames as sometimes
    # the skinkey & UI skinname differ (e.g. "standard" skinkey is
      "Classic" in the UI).
      foreach ($validSkinNames as $skinkey => & $skinname )
{
    if ( isset( $skinNames[$skinkey] ) )
{

      $skinname = $skinNames[$skinkey];
    }
}
    asort($validSkinNames);
    foreach ($validSkinNames as $skinkey => $sn )
{
    if ( in_array( $skinkey, $wgSkipSkins ) )
{

      continue;
    }
    $checked = $skinkey == $this->mSkin ? ' checked="checked"' : '';
    $mplink = htmlspecialchars($mptitle->getLocalURL(
                                    "useskin=$skinkey"));
    $previewlink = "<a target='_blank' href=\"$mplink\
                               ">$previewtext</a>";
    if( $skinkey == $wgDefaultSkin )
                        $sn .= ' (' . wfMsg( 'default' ) . ')';
    $wgOut->addHTML( "<input type='radio' name='wpSkin'
              id=\"wpSkin$skinkey\" value=\"$skinkey\"$checked />
              <label for=\"wpSkin$skinkey\">{$sn}</label>
              $previewlink<br />\n" );
    }
    $wgOut->addHTML( "</fieldset>\n\n" );
```

In order to comment out the code block, you can put /* at the beginning and */ at the end of the code block that you want to comment out. There is also an alternative way to do the same task, which is putting a # mark in front of every line that you want to comment out. The user will then not have an option to choose a skin according to his or her preferences.

Custom Navigation Bar

Sometimes it becomes necessary to change the options in the navigation bar shown on the left of the page. Suppose you want to add a new link or want to remove some unused links from there. For this we need to have the option of customizing the navigation bar as well. The easiest way to access the navigation bar page is to:

1. Put the text `MediaWiki:Sidebar` in the title field of the URL and press the *Enter* key. This will take you to the sidebar page.

2. Click the **edit** link on the page to edit the sidebar links. If you do not have the privileges to perform the task, then you have to try to change it with sysop login.

3. Once you are on the edit page, you can add, edit, or remove any link you want. Links are listed in the following format:

    ```
    ** target|caption
    ```

    Here, `target` will be replaced by the physical location of the link, and `caption` is the text that will be shown on the link. If we want to add a link to the MediaWiki home page on our navigation bar, then we have to add the following link at the end of our sidebar page.

    ```
    ** http://www.mediawiki.org|MediaWiki home
    ```

4. After that, we have to save the page and reload the page in our browser to see the effect.

Writing a New Skin

So far we have used existing skins in MediaWiki, and I know that many times you might have had the question, "Can we add our own skin in the wiki?" The answer is very straightforward. Yes, we can make our own skin from scratch and add it to the directory for the skins. In this section, we will discuss in detail how to add new skins, and how to build skins from scratch. We will follow a step-by-step procedure to build a skin. Here are the steps we need to follow when we create a new skin:

1. Design the layout for the new skin.

2. Create HTML, style properties, and integrate MediaWiki skin code.

Now let's get into the details of creating a new skin for our wiki.

Design the Layout for the New Skin

The first step in designing a skin is to visualize the skin, putting content at places of your choice. For this, it is always better to make a mental sketch of your design and then put it into place. You have to think about where to put which content, and also address what the content will look like. So let's design a new skin layout, where we will have a new type of header section where the logo, search, and general page-related links (such as **edit, discussions,** etc.) will be shown. The navigation, toolbar, and personal links (such as login, create account, preference, etc.) will be shown in the left sidebar. The layout will be similar to the following drawing:

As you can see from the drawing, we have divided our page into a few blocks to show different links and content. In the current web design scenario, a designer uses more fluid design tactics such as div-based design rather than rigid approaches such as table-based design. Div-based design gives more flexibility for designers, and for this reason, we will use div-based design to implement our layout. Let's now start implementing the HTML and style properties for the layout.

Creating HTML and Style Properties, and Integrating MediaWiki Skin Code

Before getting started with HTML and PHP code, we have to have a clear idea of the basic things that are required for a skin file. Here are few facts that we must remember:

- Every skin must have one file—the skin file, with the skin's name as the file name with a .php extension—and must also have a folder with the same name as the skin, for the CSS and image files. Suppose we want to create a new skin named haunting. Skin names are usually written as lowercase. But you have can write it in uppercase too. For our haunting skin we have to create a file named haunting.php, and a folder named haunting. Both the file and the folder must reside under skins folder of the MediaWiki installation.

- If the skin file includes or requires any file, then we have to make a separate file named skin_name.deps.php. The purpose of this file is to ensure that base classes are preloaded before compiling the skin file.

So let us create a file named haunting.php, and a folder named haunting for our new skin. In the haunting.php file, we have to include the following code:

```php
<?php

if ( !defined( 'MEDIAWIKI' ) )
  die(-1);

require_once('includes/SkinTemplate.php');

class Skinhaunting extends SkinTemplate
{
  function initPage( &$out )
    {
       SkinTemplate::initPage( $out );
       $this->skinname  = 'haunting';
       $this->stylename = 'haunting';
       $this->template  = 'hauntingTemplate';
    }
}
class hauntingTemplate extends QuickTemplate
{
  function execute()
  {
    // Suppress warnings to prevent notices about missing indexes in
    // $this->data
  wfSuppressWarnings();

  }
}
?>
```

This code extends the SkinTemplate.php class to make our new haunting skin class. The code if(!defined('MEDIAWIKI')) first checks if the call is from MediaWiki. This is for security reasons, and if the file is not called locally, the code execution will stop at this point.

In the next code block, we declare a new skin class Skinhaunting, which extends the SkinTemplate.php class. For initializing the class, we set three properties from the parent class SkinTemplate: skin name, style name, and template name.

The template name defines the template file to be used for generating the output (we have declared a new template named hauntingTemplate, which we have defined at the end). This hauntingTemplate class extends the parent class QuickTemplate and overrides the execute() function, which is called during the skin's generation. Inside the execute() function, we have to put our design and contents so that we have the desired output generated when users view the skin. Now, let us put our HTML and CSS code together, and view the results in the browser before inserting it in the execute() function:

```
<html>
<head>
<link rel="stylesheet" type="text/css" media="screen" href="/haunted/
skins/haunting/haunting.css" />
</head>
<body>
<div id="container">
  <div id="header">            <!-- start of HEADER div -->
  </div>                       <!-- end of HEADER div -->

  <div id="mBody">             <!-- start of MBODY div -->
    <div id="side">           <!-- start of SIDE div -->
    </div>                    <!-- end of SIDE div -->
    <div id="mainContent">    <!-- start of MAINCONTENT div -->
    </div>                    <!-- end of MAINCONTENT div -->
  </div>                      <!-- end of MBODY div -->

  <div id="footer">            <!-- start of FOOTER div -->
  </div>                       <!-- end of FOOTER div -->
</div>                         <!-- end of the CONTAINER div -->
</body>
</head>
</html>
```

As you can see from the code, we have added a CSS file that actually defines our style properties for the HTML tags that have been used in our design. First we built a container div, which holds all the bits and pieces together. Inside the container, we have added a header section, a main body section, and a footer section.

The main body section is further divided into two parts. The left part is designated as the sidebar. The right section is wider than the sidebar and is marked as the main content section. In order to define the width and height of the `<div>` tags and the overall layout, we have to look at the CSS file to find out the properties of the file. Here is the CSS file that we have defined for the template:

```
body  {
    min-width: 610px;
    margin: 20px;
}

#container
{
  max-width: 70em;
  margin: 0 auto;
}

#mBody
{
  clear: both;
  padding: 0 0 1em 0;
}

#side
{
  float: left;
  width: 23%;
  margin-bottom: 1em;
  border: 1px solid #000;
  height:40px;
}

#mainContent
{
  float: right;
  width: 75%;
  margin-bottom: 1em;
  border: 1px solid #000;
  height:40px;
}
#header
{
  margin-bottom: 1em;
  border: 1px solid #000;
  height:40px;
}
```

```
#footer
{
  clear: both;
  margin-top: 1em;
  border: 1px solid #000;
  height:40px;
}
```

You can see that we have defined the width of the <div> tags and their margins, and alignments, as well as a default height with a border to show on the screen. For this code, we will get an image like the following:

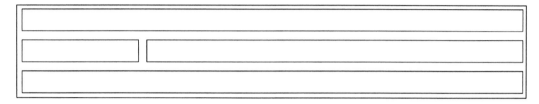

We have built the skeleton for our new skin. Now let's insert some content into it so that it looks much better than this. The hauntingTemplate class takes an associative array of data set from a SkinTemplate class and a wrapper for MediaWiki's localization database to output a formatted page. So we have to use that associative array to retrieve the required data.

Let's populate the header section:

```
function execute()
{
  wfSuppressWarnings();
  ?><!DOCTYPE html PUBLIC "-//W3C//DTD XHTML 1.0 Transitional//EN"
  "http://www.w3.org/TR/xhtml1/DTD/xhtml1-transitional.dtd">
  <html xmlns="http://www.w3.org/1999/xhtml" xml:lang="<?php $this
  >text('lang') ?>" lang="<?php $this->text('lang') ?>" dir="<?php
  $this->text('dir') ?>">
<head>
  <meta http-equiv="Content-Type" content="<?php
                                         $this->text('mimetype') ?>;
      charset=<?php $this->text('charset') ?>" />
  <?php $this->html('headlinks') ?>
  <title><?php $this->text('pagetitle') ?></title>
  <style type="text/css" media="screen,projection">
      /*<![CDATA[*/ @import "<?php $this->text('stylepath') ?>/
      <?php $this->text('stylename') ?>/main.css"; /*]]>*/
  </style>
```

```
<link rel="stylesheet" type="text/css" media="print"
  href="<?php $this->text('stylepath') ?>/common/commonPrint.css" />
<?php if($this->data['jsvarurl'  ])
{ ?>
    <script type="text/javascript" src="<?php
     $this->text('jsvarurl'  )
    ?>"></script><?php } ?>
<script type="text/javascript" src="<?php $this->text('stylepath' ) ?>
    /common/wikibits.js"></script>
<?php if($this->data['usercss'   ]) { ?><style type="text/css">
       <?php $this->html('usercss'   ) ?></style><?php    } ?>
<?php if($this->data['userjs'    ]) { ?><script type="text/
                                     javascript"
       src="<?php $this->text('userjs'    ) ?>"></script><?php } ?>
<?php if($this->data['userjsprev']) { ?><script type="text/
                                     javascript">
       <?php $this->html('userjsprev') ?></script><?php    } ?>
</head>
```

This code section defines the header for our new skin. It includes the `main.css` file from our `haunted` folder. We will see how to define the `main.css` file just a little bit later. The code section also includes a few common files such as the printing CSS file from the `common` folder in the skin directory as well as the common JavaScript file `wikibits.js`. These files are loaded if user CSS and user JavaScript is enabled. Now let's start adding the content to the body. As we already know we have to use the associative array from the `SkinTemplate` class, we will use the convention `$this->data` for the rest of the code section. We will first replace the header section code with new code and then explain what is actually going on.

```
<?php if($this->data['sitenotice']) { ?><div id="siteNotice"><?php
                        $this->html('sitenotice') ?></div><?php } ?>
<div id="header">
  <a name="top" id="contentTop"></a>
  <h1><a href="<?php echo htmlspecialchars
               ($this->data['nav_urls']['mainpage']['href'])?>"
           title="<?php $this->msg('mainpage') ?>">
           <?php $this->text('title') ?></a></h1>
  <ul>
    <?php foreach($this->data['content_actions']
                                     as $key => $action) { ?>
      <li <?php if($action['class']) { ?>class="<?php echo
           htmlspecialchars($action['class']) ?>"<?php } ?> >
```

```
            <a href="<?php echo htmlspecialchars($action['href']) ?>">
              <?php echo htmlspecialchars($action['text']) ?></a></li>
                <?php } ?>
      </ul>
      <form name="searchform" action="<?php $this->text(
                                                'searchaction') ?>"
              id="search">
          <div>
            <label for="q"><?php $this->msg('search') ?></label>
            <input id="q" name="search" type="text"
              <?php if($this->haveMsg('accesskey-search')) {?>
                    accesskey="<?php $this->msg('accesskey-search') ?>"
                    <?php } if( isset( $this->data['search'] ) ) { ?>
                    value="<?php $this->text('search') ?>"
                    <?php } ?> />
            <input type="submit" name="go" class="searchButton"
                    id="searchGoButton" value="<?php $this->msg('go')
                                                ?>" /> 
            <input type="submit" name="fulltext" class="searchButton"
                    value="<?php $this->msg('search') ?>" />
          </div>
      </form>
    </div>
```

Let's have a deeper look inside the code we've just seen. The first line checks if the site notice is enabled. If site notice is enabled then the notice will be shown at the top of the page. After that we define the header section, where we are defining an anchor for the page so that whenever you scroll down the page and click the link named **Top**, it will take you to the top of the page. The `<h1>` tag is actually defining the logo for the site with a link to the main page of the site. The `logo` property is defined in `main.css` file.

After the logo is set, we set the links for the page operation, such as **edit, discussion, history,** etc. `$this->data['content_actions']` holds all the actions defined for a particular page. After that we put the search box in the header section. Although it seems that we are putting things together and creating a code mess, the reality is different. The positioning and look of the different content will be decided by the CSS, which we will see later.

Now we will populate data in the sidebar section. The following code block loads the navigation links in the side bar. We already know the content of the navigation bar. As you can see, the navigation bar's contents are kept in the sidebar index of the associative array from the following code. Using the sidebar values we are creating links for all the available links in the sidebar.

```
<div id="side">
<?php foreach ($this->data['sidebar'] as $bar => $cont)
{ ?>
   <ul id="nav">
<li><span><?php $out = wfMsg( $bar ); if (wfEmptyMsg($bar, $out)) echo
                                $bar; else echo $out; ?></span>
<?php       foreach($cont as $key => $val)
{ ?>
<li id="<?php echo htmlspecialchars($val['id']) ?>"<?php
if ( $val['active'] ) { ?> class="active" <?php }
?>><a href="<?php echo htmlspecialchars($val['href']) ?>"><?php echo
                           htmlspecialchars($val['text']) ?></a></li>
<?php        } ?>
</ul>
<?php } ?>
```

The following code populates the personal URL section links, such as **create an account/login, logout, my preferences, my watchlist, my talk**, etc.

```
<ul id="nav">
<li><span><?php $this->msg('personaltools') ?></span>
<?php foreach($this->data['personal_urls'] as $key => $item)
{
?><li id="pt-<?php echo htmlspecialchars($key) ?>"><a href="<?php
echo htmlspecialchars($item['href']) ?>"<?php
if(!empty($item['class']))
{ ?>
class="<?php
           echo htmlspecialchars($item['class']) ?>"<?php } ?>><?php
           echo htmlspecialchars($item['text']) ?></a></li><?php
} ?>
</ul>
```

The following code populates the toolbox section of the sidebar. The common links in the toolbox section such as recent changes, what links here, upload files, special pages, etc. are loaded.

```
<ul id="nav">
<li><span><?php $this->msg('toolbox') ?></span>
           <?php if($this->data['notspecialpage']) { foreach( array(
           'whatlinkshere', 'recentchangeslinked' ) as $special )
{ ?>
<li id="t-<?php echo $special?>"><a href="<?php
     echo htmlspecialchars($this->data['nav_urls'][$special]['href'])
     ?>"><?php echo $this->msg($special) ?></a></li>
<?php }
```

```
} ?>
<?php if($this->data['feeds'])
{ ?><li id="feedlinks"><?php foreach($this->data['feeds']
                                              as $key => $feed)
{
?><span id="feed-<?php echo htmlspecialchars($key) ?>"><a href="<?php
echo htmlspecialchars($feed['href']) ?>"><?php echo htmlspecialchars($
feed['text'])?></a> </span>
<?php } ?></li><?php } ?>
<?php foreach( array('contributions', 'emailuser', 'upload',
'specialpages') as $special )
{ ?>
<?php if($this->data['nav_urls'][$special])
{?><li id="t-<?php echo $special ?>"><a href="<?php
     echo htmlspecialchars($this->data['nav_urls'][$special]['href'])
     ?>"><?php $this->msg($special) ?></a></li><?php } ?>
<?php } ?>
</ul>
```

The last addition to the sidebar is the language URLs. If multiple languages are supported on the site, then this code will show the supported languages' links in the sidebar just below the toolbox section.

```
<?php if( $this->data['language_urls'] )
{ ?>
<ul id="nav">
<li><span><?php $this->msg('otherlanguages') ?></span>
<?php foreach($this->data['language_urls'] as $langlink)
{ ?>
<li>
<a href="<?php echo htmlspecialchars($langlink['href'])
?>"><?php echo $langlink['text'] ?></a>
</li>
<?php } ?>
</ul>
<?php } ?>
</div><!-- end of SIDE div -->
```

Next we will populate the main content section of the page, which can be done using the following code:

```
<div id="mainContent">
    <h1><?php $this->text('title') ?></h1>
    <h3 id="siteSub"><?php $this->msg('tagline') ?></h3>
    <div id="contentSub"><?php $this->html('subtitle') ?></div>
    <?php if($this->data['undelete']) { ?><div id="contentSub">
```

```
        <?php        $this->html('undelete') ?></div><?php } ?>
    <?php if($this->data['newtalk'] ) { ?><div class="usermessage">
        <?php $this->html('newtalk')   ?></div><?php } ?>
    <!-- start content -->
    <?php $this->html('bodytext') ?>
    <?php if($this->data['catlinks']) { ?><div id="catlinks">
        <?php $this->html('catlinks') ?></div><?php } ?>
    <!-- end content -->
    </div><!-- end of MAINCONTENT div -->
```

The code is pretty straightforward and also similar to what we have seen when we modified the MonoBook.php file. The basic difference will be made by the layout of the divs and the style that we apply to them. Now let's finish the code for haunting. php by adding the code for the footer section. Here it is:

```
<div id="footer">
  <table><tr>
    <td align="left" width="1%" nowrap="nowrap">
      <?php if($this->data['copyrightico']) {
                              ?><div id="f-copyrightico">
          <?php $this->html('copyrightico') ?></div><?php } ?></td>
    <td align="center">
      <?php if($this->data['lastmod'   ]) { ?><span id="f-lastmod">
          <?php $this->html('lastmod')     ?></span><?php } ?>
      <?php if($this->data['viewcount' ]) { ?><span id="f-viewcount">
          <?php  $this->html('viewcount')  ?> </span><?php } ?>
      <ul id="f-list">
        <?php if($this->data['credits'  ]) { ?><li id="f-credits">
            <?php $this->html('credits')    ?></li><?php } ?>
        <?php if($this->data['copyright' ]) { ?><li id="f-copyright">
            <?php  $this->html('copyright')  ?></li><?php } ?>
        <?php if($this->data['about'     ]) { ?><li id="f-about">
            <?php $this->html('about')       ?></li><?php } ?>
        <?php if($this->data['disclaimer']) { ?><li id="f-disclaimer">
            <?php $this->html('disclaimer') ?></li><?php } ?>
      </ul>
    </td>
    <td align="right" width="1%" nowrap="nowrap">
      <?php if($this->data['poweredbyico']) { ?>
          <div id="f-poweredbyico"><?php $this->html('poweredbyico') ?>
          </div><?php } ?></td>
  </tr></table>
</div>
```

We are now done with structuring the layout with new code based on the skin template data. However, we haven't seen the CSS for this defined structure. The CSS for this skin will be so huge that it would take pages to describe each of the CSS files.

Instead of doing so, we will see a few of the CSS properties. The complete CSS files will be available for download from `http://www.packtpub.com` as a complete skin download. So here are a few CSS properties defined for the skin's header section:

```css
/* Header */

#header
{
  background: #455372 url("header_bl.png") bottom left repeat-x;
  position: relative;
  min-height: 39px;
  height: 5em;
  padding: 0;
  height: 3em;
  padding: 15px 0;
}

#header h1
{
  position: absolute;
  top: 0;
  left: 0;
  margin: 0;
  font-size: 2px;
  background: url("header_tl.gif") no-repeat;
  height: 8px;
  z-index: 100; /* above the UL */
}

#header h1 a
{
  display: block;
  width: 268px;
  height: 64px;
  background: transparent url("header_logo.gif") no-repeat;
  text-indent: -700em;
  text-decoration: none;
}

#header ul
{
  width: auto;
  position: absolute;
  bottom: 0;
  right: -1;
```

```
      margin: 0;
      padding: 0 15px 0 0;
      list-style: none;
      background: url("header_br.gif") no-repeat bottom right;
      z-index: 90; /* below the H1 */
    }

      #header li
    {
      float: right;
      background: transparent url("header_tab.gif") 100% -600px no-repeat;
      padding: 0 6px 0 0;
      margin: 0 1px 0 0;
      border-bottom: 1px solid #515358;
    }

      #header ul a
    {
      float: left;
      display: block;
      padding: 4px 4px 4px 10px;
      background: transparent url("header_tab.gif") 0% -600px no-repeat;
      font-weight: bold;
      color: #fff;
      text-decoration: none;
    }

      #header ul li:hover a
    {
      background-position: 0% -400px;
    }

      #header ul li:hover
    {
      background-position: 100% -400px;
    }

    /* Search Field */

      #header form
    {
      width:auto;
      position: absolute;
      top: 0;
      right: -1;
      padding: 12px 20px 0 0;
```

```
  background: url("header_tr.gif") no-repeat top right;
  margin: 0; /* need for IE Mac */
  text-align: right; /* need for IE Mac */
  white-space: nowrap; /* for Opera */
}


#header form label { color: #fff; font-size: 85%; }
#header form input { font-size: 85%; }

#header form #submit
{
  font-size: 85%;
  background: #6A7389;
  color: #fff;
  padding: 1px 4px;
  border-right: 1px solid #283043;
  border-bottom: 1px solid #283043;
  border-top: 1px solid #9097A2;
  border-left: 1px solid #9097A2;
}


#header form #q
{
  width: 170px;
  font-size: 85%;
  border: 1px solid #9097A2;
  background: #D9DBE1;
  padding: 2px;
}


#header form #q:hover, #header form #q:focus
{
  background: #fff;
}
```

The final result of the skin can be seen in the following screenshot. You just need to enable the skin from your user preference or make it the default for your site for it to take effect.

We have changed the look of our wiki site by making a new layout and defining new style properties for the tags we have used. By applying this knowledge, you can create any type of skin you want. You have the liberty to pick and choose which options you want to retain in the skin, and which ones to omit.

> All the files, including the CSS and the images, will be available for download from the Packt Publishing website http://www.packtpub.com. You can download the skin file to your skins folder and work with it the way you want.

Summary

In this chapter we learned many aspects of customizing MediaWiki. We now know how to change the appearance as well as the layout of the site. We know how to change the look of the site by changing the CSS file as well as by changing the core code blocks. We also learned how we can design a new skin for our wiki.

All the way it was a very informative chapter and also a little bit advanced for newbies. However, it is always nice to play with things that attract you more. Start working with the skin design for MediaWiki, and you will find that you can make your site look better by doing so. In the next chapter, our focus will be on extending MediaWiki features i.e. hacking, and we will explore the core code base of MediaWiki in the next chapter for this.

9
Hacking MediaWiki

Hacking MediaWiki is the process of changing the MediaWiki code base to suit our needs. A hacker is a person who creates and modifies or hacks software, or reaches a goal by employing a series of modifications to exploit or extend existing code or resources. Though the word hacking has negative impact in various societies, not all hackers have bad intentions. A positive meaning of "hacker" can be someone who knows a set of programming interfaces well enough to write software rapidly and expertly. We will take this definition for our purpose. We will learn how to modify or add features to MediaWiki rapidly by understanding the internal structure and interfaces.

The File Structure

We already know that MediaWiki is built on PHP and MySQL. So in order to add or modify anything in MediaWiki, we need to have sound knowledge of PHP and MySQL. So far we have applied our basic PHP knowledge in the `LocalSettings.php` file, but now we need to apply more of our knowledge to edit the existing code base, and also a bit of patience to work on it. Let's look at the core MediaWiki files, some of which will be modifies as required:

File Name	Description
index.php	This is the main entry point to the application. This page redirects to other pages based on the passed parameters.
Article.php	This page contains code for viewing, deleting, watching, and unwatching a page. It also contains basic functions responsible for a part of the editing functionality, such as fetching a revision and saving a page.
	When we edit a page, all article-related information such as article name, article contents, etc., are provided by the Article.php file. Database and text operations are done through the Article.php file as well.

File Name	Description
EditPage.php	This page contains code for editing a page. A part of the editing, however, is handled by the Article.php file.
Parser.php	This page contains the code for parsing wiki syntax to HTML tags.
Linker.php	This page contains code for generating HTML code for links and images.
Database.php	This page contains all the functions for separate database operation.
OutputPage.php	This page is used as output buffer. All the text is sent to this class before being shown on screen or in other media.
Title.php	As the name suggests, this page is solely responsible for displaying and saving page titles.
User.php	This page contains the user-related code—especially code sections for user preference and permission.
Setup.php	This page initializes all variables used in MediaWiki. A part of the initialization also involves the global variables and objects.
Default Settings.php	This page contains the default values for all the variables used in MediaWiki. If some values need to be changed or redefined, they are defined in the LocalSettings.php file.

Now we know which files exist and what they do. So it is better to study these files very well before making any changes. Though the code is not very well organized, you can still make out some meaning by reading the contents.

MediaWiki Hooks

In MediaWiki, we can attach functionality to events. This is known as hooking. The sole purpose of doing this is to execute our own functionality after selected events. MediaWiki provides several hooks to extend the MediaWiki functionality. For example, if you want to set up a new type of user login procedure in your system, then you might be interested in hooking your own implementation with MediaWiki's existing code. In MediaWiki, a hook is defined as:

A hook is a clump of code and data that should run when an event happens. This can be either a function and a chunk of data, or an object and a method.

MediaWiki hooks allow hackers, third-party developers, and site administrators to define new functionality that will run at a certain point of time in the mainline code. The best thing about a hook is that you don't have to change the actual code section of MediaWiki and still can achieve your goal by adding different hooks for different events. Hooks give us the option to keep the mainline code clean, and create new extension very easily. Hooks are very good alternatives to local patches. Hook modifications are kept separately (usually in the extensions folders) so that they do not create any problem with the mainline code.

Every MediaWiki hook must be associated with an event followed by the action to be performed upon occurrence of the event. An event is something that happens on the wiki. An event can occur when a user logs in to the system, a wiki page is created, a wiki page is saved, a wiki page deleted, etc. Every event must be named. A few existing event names in MediaWiki are `ArticleDelete`, `ArticleSave`, and `ArticleFromTitle`. We can use the existing events available in MediaWiki or we can add new events based on our need.

Now, we know that a hook is a chunk of code run at some particular event and can perform some action. Usually the action is either a function or an object. A function can have optional data to perform some operation. The object can have an optional method name and optional data to perform an operation when the event occurs. Hooks are registered when they are added to the global `$wgHooks` array for a given event. The `$wgHooks` variable is located in the `includes/DefaultSettings.php` file. In order to add new hooks, we have to add those hooks at the end of the `LocaltSettings.php` file. The following code section describes how we can create a hook and assign a function for it:

```
$wgHooks['EventName'][] = 'functionName';
$wgHooks['EventName'][] = array('functionName', $functionData);
```

The first line will create a hook for the provided event name, and this hook will call the assigned function when the event occurs. The second line is similar to the first one except that on the occurrence of the event, the function will be called with some data. Usually function name and data kept in an array as shown above. When an event occurs, the function will be called with the optional data provided as well as event-specific parameters. The previous examples would result in the following code being executed when `'EventName'` takes place:

```
# function, no data
functionName ($functionParameter)
# function with data
functionName ($functionData, $functionParameter)
```

We can also assign an object to a hook instead of a function. The following code section describes it:

```
$wgHooks['EventName'][] = $object;
$wgHooks['EventName'][] = array($object, 'methodName');
$wgHooks['EventName'][] = array($object, 'methodName', $methodData);
```

The first line will create a hook for the provided event name, and this hook will call the assigned object when the event occurs. The second will create a hook for an object with a method name. So when that particular event occurs, the provided method of the object will be executed. The third line takes optional data for the hook. When the particular event occurs, the object method will be called with the optional data as well as event-specific parameters provided. The previous examples would result in the following code being executed when `'EventName'` occurs:

```
# object only
$object->onEventName($methodParameter)
# object with method
$object->methodName($methodParameter)
# object with method and data
$object->methodName($methodData, $methodParameter)
```

Note that when an object is the hook and there is no specified method, the default method called is `onEventName()`. For different events this would be different; for example, if the event name is `ArticleSave`, the `onArticleSave()` method will be automatically called, and for the `ArticleDelete` event, the `onArticleDelete()` method will be called, and so on.

The extra data is useful if we want to use the same function or object for different purposes. Consider:

```
$wgHooks['ArticleChanged'][] = array('emailNotify', 'Author');
$wgHooks['ArticleChanged'][] = array('emailNotify', 'Admin');
```

This code would result in `emailNotify` being run twice when an article is changed: once for `'Author'`, and once for `'Admin'`.

Hooks can return three possible values:

- **True**: The hook has operated successfully.
- **False**: The hook has successfully done the work required of it, and the calling function should skip. In this case the hook function basically replaces main functionality. So if the hook returns false, it means that the hook has performed the required task and as a result the main functionality is not required to execute.
- **Error string**: An error has occurred; the processing should stop and the error be returned to the user.

Using Hooks

A calling function or method uses the `wfRunHooks()` function to run the hooks related to a particular event. The function is located in the `includes/Hooks.php` file. The `wfRunHooks()` function takes two parameters. The first parameter is the event name, and second parameter contains the hook parameters such as function name with data or object with method name and data.

A call of the function might look like the following:

```
wfRunHooks('ArticleProtectComplete',
                    array(&$this,$wgUser,$limit,$reason));
```

`wfRunHooks()` returns true if the calling function should continue processing (the hooks ran OK, or that there are no hooks to run), or false if it shouldn't continue.

From the MediaWiki site, you can get a complete list of available hooks. Not all hooks will work on your version. If your version is old, make sure that the hook is compatible with your installed version. For this, you can look for the version number at the beginning of each hook description. The URL for the MediaWiki hooks is `http://www.mediawiki.org/wiki/Help:MediaWiki_hooks`.

If you want to add any hook, it will be better to know the events available in MediaWiki. Here is a list of known events in MediaWiki:

Event Name	Description
AddNewAccount	After a user account is created
ArticleDelete	Before an article is deleted
ArticleDeleteComplete	After an article is deleted
ArticleProtect	Before an article is protected
ArticleProtectComplete	After an article is protected
ArticleSave	Before an article is saved
ArticleSaveComplete	After an article is saved
BlockIp	Before an IP address or user is blocked
BlockIpComplete	After an IP address or user is blocked
EmailUser	Before sending email from one user to another
EmailUserComplete	After sending email from one user to another
LogPageValidTypes	Action being logged
LogPageLogName	Name of the logging page
LogPageLogHeader	Strings used by `wfMsg` as a header
TitleMoveComplete	After moving an article
UnknownAction	An unknown "action" has occurred
UnwatchArticle	Before a watch is removed from an article
UserLoginComplete	After a user has logged in
UserLogout	Before a user logs out
UserLogoutComplete	After a user has logged out
WatchArticle	Before a watch is added to an article
WatchArticleComplete	After a watch is added to an article
CategoryPageView	Before viewing a categorypage in `CategoryPage::view`

Extending Wiki Markup

We have seen in earlier chapters how easy MediaWiki syntax can be. We have also seen that many HTML tags are supported by MediaWiki. The most exciting feature of MediaWiki is that we can add our own markup into the MediaWiki system. So we can create custom markup tags for special purposes.

Suppose we want to create a new tag named <GHOSTNOTE>, which will show an author's note in a rectangular box with a different background color every time the user visits the page. So if you see the background of the note next time, it might be a different color. There are different ways of adding markup to MediaWiki. One way is to add the markup as an extension, which is a common way of achieving this task. Another way of adding markup is by adding the markup hook in the Setup.php file; this reduces the necessity of creating your own extension. We will use the latter approach for our goal.

We will add support for a new tag, which is in the format of <GHOSTNOTE> </GHOSTNOTE >. In order to support this tag, we have to add the following code section at the end of the includes/Setup.php file, before the end tag (?>):

```
function ParseGHOSTNOTETag($Content)
{
  global $wgOut;
  $wgOut->enableClientCache(false);
  $Content = str_replace("<GHOSTNOTE>", "", $Content);
  $Content = str_replace("</GHOSTNOTE>", "", $Content);
  $randomColor = rand(0,9);
  $bgColor = array ( '#CCCCFF', '#FFCCFF', '#FFCCCC',
      '#33CCFF', '#33CCCC', '#FFFFCC', '#99CCFF',
      '#FF9933', '#99FF99',  '#FF6699');
  $returnStr="<center><table width=50% border=1 style='border: .75pt
      dashed white; background-color: ".$bgColor[$randomColor]."'>
      <tr><td align=center valign=middle bgcolor="$bgColor
      [$randomColor]"><pre>";
  $returnStr .= $Content;
  $returnStr .=  "</pre></td></tr></table></center>";
  return $returnStr;
}
$wgParser->setHook('GHOSTNOTE','ParseGHOSTNOTETag');
```

Now let us get a complete picture of what this function is doing. This function parses our defined tag using our defined method. The $wgOut object is responsible for the output generated by MediaWiki. We are using the global $wgOut object instead of creating a new object. By doing so, we can use the same object that is used by other functions and classes in the server.

After that we set the `enableClientCache()` method to be false. This will force the server to send non-cacheable headers to the client; as a result, the page with our tag won't be cached in client's machine, and every time he or she wants to see that page, a fresh copy will be sent from the server. After that the content inside the tags is obtained by eliminating the start and end tag from the supplied text.

A random color is then chosen from our color array with the help of a random index generator, to display as background color for the notes. In the `$returnStr` variable, we put the tag contents inside a table with a random background color, and then return it to the parser class as a parsed output of the tag. We have the freedom to perform whatever task we want with the content. Here we have shown the text in a better formatted manner. Now we have to save the file and open any page and write the following lines with our new tag:

```
<GHOSTNOTE>
   Main Page is under construction.
   We are trying to improve the quality of the Graphics.

   Thanks for your Support
   Administrator
   Haunted Site
</GHOSTNOTE>
```

If we save the page after writing these lines, we will see the following image. If you refresh the browser, you will see that the color of the border changes. So for different users, the box color will be different. This can be a very useful tag to catch visitor's attention.

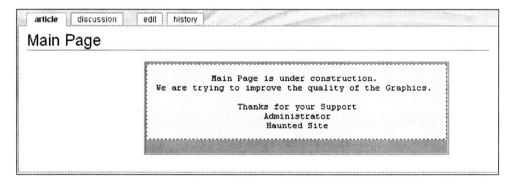

We have extended our wiki markup very easily. So far our hacking session is going well, but don't feel that you have learned a lot. Watch out for the next section—we will be writing our own pages, and our own code sections.

Article Rating: A Cool Hack

In our haunted site, we have a lot of stories published, and more coming every day, but how do we know how people are reacting to these stories, articles, etc.? We don't have any way to measure the user reaction for each post. To deal with this, we can implement a rating system for articles and stories to show the site's users how the articles have been rated, and provide them with the ability to rate the articles themselves. So let us make a quick requirement note of the features we will be adding:

- A rating message such as "average rating of this article is xx (out of xx) after xx ratings" will be shown for the ratings earned so far by that article.
- A rating form where visitors can rank stories from a level of 1 (low) to 5 (high).
- Only the article view page will have the ratings form enabled.
- The ratings result for the article will be shown, unless the article is the main page.
- Only logged-in users should be able to rate.
- A user can rate an article only once.

First let us decide what type of change we will be making and how many tables will have to be added in the database. To make it in a simple manner without altering existing code, we will add the following tables:

- One table, `articleRating`, for storing ratings for each article based on the article number
- One table, `articleRatingHistory`, for storing ratings history

Since we know the task we are looking at performing, let's get to work. First we create the required table in the database.

The `articleRating` table will have the following fields:

- `articleID` to hold the article number
- `articleName` to hold the article name
- `totalRatings` to hold the number of ratings
- `totalPoints` to hold total ratings points

The `articleRatingHistory` table will have the following fields:

- `articleID` to hold the article number
- `userName` to hold user names
- `articleRating` to hold the user's rating

Next we have to create the tables in the database using SQL syntax. We can do it either by directly logging in to the MySQL server or through phpMyAdmin. Since most of the hosted servers prefer using phpMyAdmin, we will see how to use phpMyAdmin to create our tables. Here is the SQL command to create the tables:

```
CREATE TABLE `articlerating`
   (`articleID` INT NOT NULL , `articleName` VARCHAR( 250 ) NOT
      NULL, `totalRatings` INT NOT NULL, `totalPoints` INT NOT NULL,
      PRIMARY KEY ( `articleID` ));

CREATE TABLE `articleratinghistory`
   (`articleID` INT NOT NULL , `userName` VARCHAR( 50 ) NOT
      NULL , `articleRating` TINYINT NOT NULL );
```

 If a database table prefix has been defined for the wiki, then we have to add the table prefix in front of the table name in the previous SQL in order to create the new tables. $wgDBprefix in the LocalSettings. php file contains the prefix value. It is necessary to add the prefix before creating any new tables in the database server.

We have to write the SQL command in our PhpMyadmin SQL query window and execute the command by pressing the **Go** button. This will create the two new tables in our database. After doing so we are done with designing and implementing the database part.

We have to move our focus now to coding using PHP. In order to understand the code section easily, we will follow a step-by-step procedure to achieve our goal.

1. First of all we have to extend our functionality, and in order to do so, we have to add our extension. Let us call our extension file RateArticle. php; we will be adding our required functionalities to this file. As we have discussed in the requirement phase, we will show a rating message if the article is already rated by the user, and if the user is logged in, we will show the rating form to get that particular user's rating. Here is the code section that performs this task. Let us add the code to our newly created RateArticle.php file.

    ```php
    <?
    if ( ! defined( 'MEDIAWIKI' ) )
    die();
    require_once("DatabaseFunctions.php");
    function wfRateArticleForm()
    {
      global $wgArticle, $wgUser, $wgScriptPath;
    ```

```
if(isset($_GET['rated']) && $_GET['rated'] == "successfully")
{
  $wgArticle->purge();
}
$s  = getArticleRating();
if($wgUser->isLoggedIn())
{
  if(!articleRated())
  {
    $s .= '<form name="rank" class="inline" method="post"
            action="'.$wgScriptPath.'/saverating.php">'"
    <br> Rate this Article:
            <input type=radio name=rating value=1> 1
            <input type=radio name=rating value=2> 2
            <input type=radio name=rating value=3 checked> 3
            <input type=radio name=rating value=4> 4
            <input type=radio name=rating value=5> 5
    <Br>
    <input type=hidden name=articleID value='
      ".wgArticle->getID()."'>"."<input type=hidden name
      =articleTitle value='".$wgArticle->getTitle()->
      getPrefixedText()."'>"."<input type=hidden name=userName
      value='".$wgUser->getName()."'>". '<input type="submit"
      name="go" value="Save your Rating" /> </form>';
  }
}
echo $s;
}
```

The first line of the code checks if MEDIAWIKI is defined; this is just a security measure. If MEDIAWIKI is not defined, then it indicates that the call might not be initiated by our wiki server and the script will stop execution at this point. If MEDIAWIKI is defined, then the script will continue to execute the rest of the functionality.

In the next line we are required to include a file named DatabaseFunctions. php, which will be used for all the database functionality. If the file is not found, then the code will throw an exception and stop execution.

After that we have declared a function named wfRateArticleForm. This is the function responsible for showing the rating form and the message. Inside this function, we have used the global declaration of the article and user variable in order to access the article-related information such as article ID and name, as well as user-related information such as whether the user is logged in, his or her user name, etc.

Next, we have added a condition to check if the article rating is saved successfully or not. If the rating has been added successfully, we force the server to delete the cached page for this article and load the new version of the page, as the page has been updated with ratings. The `$wgArticle->purge()` function performs the desired task for us.

Now we have to show the ratings earned so far by this article. In order to do so, we will be using another function, `getArticleRating()`, which will return a message with the average rating for this article and the number of ratings, or a message to inform the user that this article has not been rated so far. We know the basic mechanism of the function, but we haven't seen the code for it yet. We will implement that functionality in the next step.

Now we check if the user is logged in, with the help of the function `$wgUser->isLoggedIn()`. If the user is logged in, then we check if the user has already rated this article. For this, we will use our own implemented function `articleRated()`, which will return true if the article has been rated by this user previously, and false otherwise. If the article has not been rated yet by the user, then it will show a form with five radio box buttons (showing digits from 1 to 5, i.e. the rating options) and a save button. In this form, we will be passing the article ID, the title, and the user name as hidden fields so that the server gets the information about the user who rated the article, and also gets the article information. The page information will be saved by a page named `saverating.php` as mentioned in the form property.

2. We will now add the functionality for showing the article rating string for a particular article. In the previous section we talked about the `getArticleRating()` function, which will return the rating string for the article. Here is the implementation of that function:

```
function getArticleRating()
{
    global $wgArticle, $wgDBprefix;
    $articleID = $wgArticle->getID();
    $totalRatings  = 0;
    $totalPoints   = 0;
    $averageRating = 0;
    $sql = "SELECT totalRatings, totalPoints FROM {$wgDBprefix}
                        articlerating WHERE articleID=$articleID" ;
    $res = wfQuery( $sql, DB_READ );
    if( $s = wfFetchObject( $res ) )
    {
        $totalRatings = $s->totalRatings;
        $totalPoints  = $s->totalPoints;
    }
    if($totalRatings>0)
```

```
  {
    $averageRating = $totalPoints/$totalRatings;
    return "Average Rating for this Article is
           <b>".sprintf "%.2f",$averageRating)."</b>
           ( out of 5.00 ) after $totalRatings Ratings";
  }
  else
  {
    return "No rating has been done for this Article.";
  }
}
```

In this functionality, we are querying the database in order to find the total ratings earned for this article (we are querying our newly created table `articlerating`). In the SQL query, we have added `$wgDBprefix` in front of our table name so that if the database has a table prefix name defined, then it will add the prefix in front of the table name to execute properly.

We are using a few MediaWiki-defined database functionalities in order to perform the task. The `wfQuery` function runs an SQL query and returns a result set for the executed query, and `wfFetchObject` fetches objects from the result set. The rest of the code is self-explanatory, as we can see that if there is any rating provided, we are calculating the average rating and showing it as a string, or are showing no rating information if the article is yet to be rated.

3. Now we have to add our last functionality to the extension, which is `articleRated()`. This function will return true if the user has already rated the article, and false otherwise. Here is the code for this functionality:

```
function articleRated()
{
  global $wgArticle, $wgUser, $wgDBprefix;
  $articleID = $wgArticle->getID();
  $userName  = $wgUser->getName();
  $sql = "SELECT * FROM {$wgDBprefix}articleratinghistory WHERE
               articleID=$articleID and userName = '$userName'" ;
  $res = wfQuery( $sql, DB_READ );
  if( $s = wfFetchObject( $res ) )
  {
    return true;
  }
  else
  {
    return false;
  }
}
```

As we can see, we are querying the `articleratinghistory` table to find out whether the user has already rated the article.

4. Save the `RateArticle.php` file and put it inside the `extensions` folder of the wiki installation.

5. Our next step will be to add a hook for the implemented function. In order to do so, we have to add the following line at the end of our `LocalSettings.php` file in the root folder of the wiki installation. This hook runs when an event named `AfterArticleDisplayed` occurs:

```
$wgHooks['AfterArticleDisplayed'][] = 'wfRateArticleForm';
```

6. After this we have to add our extension file at the end of `LocalSettings.php`. The following code needs to be added for this purpose:

```
require_once("extensions/RateArticle.php");
```

7. We have defined our hook for the extended functionality, and we now need to show this functionality to the user. To implement this, we have to modify our skin file. So let's open our default skin file `MonoBook.php` file from the `skins` directory. In the file, try to find the footer code blocks, which start with the following code:

```
<div class="visualClear"></div>
<div id="footer">
```

and add the following code section just before the mentioned code section:

```
<?
global $wgTitle, $wgOut;
if($wgOut->isArticle() && $wgTitle->getArticleId()>1)
{
   ?>
   <div class="visualClear"></div>
   <div id="footer">
   <? wfRunHooks( 'AfterArticleDisplayed'); ?>
   </div>
   <?
}
?>
```

This code section checks if the page we are now loading is an article page. If it is an article page, then we check whether it is the main page. If it is an article page and not the main page, then we run our hook to show the newly added rating section. To test this functionality, save the page and open an article page in the wiki other than the main page.

You will see the following change in the display:

| article | discussion | edit | history |

Story

Let share a story about a **Ghost** in a small village near **Michigan**

The story of the *Crying Girl* [edit]

The village name is known as ghost village. People say that there is a ghost near the river bank that appears every midnight. Some people have reported seeing her.

"She is around 14 years old. She always wears a white dress and she holds a little doll in her hand."

.says a person from the village who claims to have seen the girl several times.

It is said that the girl drowned in the river a long time ago while crossing the river by boat with family members. Everyone in the boat died. The girl lost her younger brother in this accident. His body was never found. That's why she comes out every night to find her lost brother.

No rating has been done for this Article.

This means that our hook has run properly, and the appropriate message has been shown, as no rating has been done for this article yet. The form is not shown yet, since we are not logged in. Let us now log in to the system and find out what is actually happening:

| article | discussion | edit | history | protect | delete | move | watch |

Story

Let share a story about a **Ghost** in a small village near **Michigan**

The story of the *Crying Girl* [edit]

The village name is known as ghost village. People say that there is a ghost near the river bank that appears every midnight. Some people have reported seeing her.

"She is around 14 years old. She always wears a white dress and she holds a little doll in her hand."

.says a person from the village who claims to have seen the girl several times.

It is said that the girl drowned in the river a long time ago while crossing the river by boat with family members. Everyone in the boat died. The girl lost her younger brother in this accident. His body was never found. That's why she comes out every night to find her lost brother.

No rating has been done for this Article.

Rate this Article: ○ 1 ○ 2 ◉ 3 ○ 4 ○ 5

[Save your Rating]

Once we have logged in, we see the rating form for a particular article that has not been rated yet. But wait; we cannot rate this article now. Since we have not implemented our saverating.php file, nothing will happen when we rate the article and click the **Save your Rating** button. We have to create the file and save it in the root folder of our installation. Here is the code for saverating.php:

```
require_once( './includes/WebStart.php' );
$dbw =& wfGetDB( DB_MASTER );
$dbw->begin();
```

The first line declares the default MediaWiki files for database operation. The second line is responsible for getting the database for the write operation. DB_MASTER defines that the database operation is a write operation. In MediaWiki, DB_SLAVE is used for read-only operations and DB_MASTER for database write operations. The third line declares the start of the database transaction.

We are now ready to write our SQL operations. First we will try to update the articlerating table to add the ratings for the particular article. If the update operation does not affect any rows, then we have to assume that the article has not been rated so far, and we need to insert the first rating. Here is the code section for this:

```
$sql = "update {$wgDBprefix}articlerating set
            `totalRatings` = `totalRatings` + 1,
            `totalPoints`  = `totalPoints` + '$_POST[rating]'
            where `articleID` = '$_POST[articleID]' ";
$res = $dbw->query($sql);
if($dbw->affectedRows()==0)
{
  $sql = "insert into {$wgDBprefix}articlerating set
              `articleID`    = '$_POST[articleID]',
              `articleName`  = '$_POST[articleTitle]',
              `totalRatings` = 1,
              `totalPoints`  = '$_POST[rating]' ";
  $res = $dbw->query( $sql );
}
```

Next, we have to add the rating to the rating history table in order to store information about the user who rated the article as well as the information about the article itself. After doing so, we will return to the article page with a success message in the URL, which will tell the server to reload the newer version of the page as we have discussed in step 1 of this section.

```
$sql = "insert into {$wgDBprefix}articleratinghistory set
            `articleID`     = '$_POST[articleID]',
            `userName`   = '$_POST[userName]',
            `articleRating` = '$_POST[rating]'";
```

```
$res = $dbw->query( $sql );
$dbw->commit();
header("Location: index.php?title=".$_POST
        ['articleTitle']."&rated=successfully");
```

The preceding code section shows that we are inserting all rating information to our history table, and after running all the queries, we are committing the transaction to take effect. At the last line, we are moving our page to the article page with a success message.

Now let us rate one article and see what happens:

| article | discussion | edit | history | protect | delete | move | watch |

Story

Let share a story about a **Ghost** in a small village near **Michigan**

The story of the *Crying Girl* [edit]

The village name is known as `ghost village`. People say that there is a ghost near the river bank that appears every midnight. Some people have reported seeing her.

`"She is around 14 years old. She always wears a white dress and she holds a little doll in her hand."`

says a person from the village who claims to have seen the girl several times.

It is said that the girl drowned in the river a long time ago while crossing the river by boat with family members. Everyone in the boat died. The girl lost her younger brother in this accident. His body was never found. That's why she comes out every night to find her lost brother.

Average Rating for this Article is **5.00** (out of 5.00) after 1 Ratings

This shows that we have implemented the article rating hack properly. We have learned about hooks, extensions, and how to use them in our code without changing the core code base much. We have hacked MediaWiki, and for a good purpose. Now we can see our article's ratings and know if it is catching our readers' attention. We don't, however, have a way to see how all our articles are getting rated. Going through article after article will be a hard and time-consuming task. How about having a page where we can see all the articles' ratings (such as all pages in the special page section)? We can make one special page for this purpose, and we are going to see how we can write a new special page.

Writing a New Special Page

So we are up to write a new special page for our haunted site, where people can view article ratings. We will show the article name, current ratings, and the total number of ratings received for each of the rated articles. Writing a special page in MediaWiki is very easy. We can extend our MediaWiki functionality by adding special pages according to our need.

Our main goal here will be to create an includable special page that will be listed by default for all users. When a user visits this special page, a default list of 50 articles will be shown with the current average rating and the total number of ratings for each article. Users will have the option to choose the list size to be 10, 20, 30, 50, 100, and 150 articles.

> In the `includes/SpecialPage.php` file, we have all special pages listed in an array. If we look at the code for all special pages listed in the `$mList` array, we will see that there are mainly three types of special pages declared.
>
> The first type is the general `SpecialPage`, which is generally listed and can not be included. These special pages are listed in the special page section, and we can view them from the list. Another type of special page is the `UnlistedSpecialPage`, which is not listed in the special pages list. These pages are plain files that are used directly by the system. Examples of such special pages are the logout page, special pages list, contributions, the move page, etc. The remaining special page type, `IncludableSpecialPage`, creates a special page that is includable via the syntax: `{{special:pagename}}`. Recent changes, new pages, and all pages are all includable. This type of special page is also listed by default.

Now we have to write a special page that will fetch the `articlerating` table from the database and show us the article names, ratings, etc. The following code does exactly this for us. We have to save this code inside the `extensions` folder as `SpecialPageRating.php`:

```php
<?php
if( defined( 'MEDIAWIKI' ) )
{
   require_once( 'SpecialPage.php' );
   $wgExtensionFunctions[] = 'wfSpecialPageRating';
   $wgExtensionCredits['specialpage'][] = array( 'name' =>
      'Article Ratings', 'author' => 'Mizanur Rahman', 'url' => '' );
   function wfSpecialPageRating()
   {
      global $wgMessageCache;
```

```
SpecialPage::addPage( new PageRating() );
$wgMessageCache->addMessage( 'pagerating', 'Article Ratings' );
$wgMessageCache->addMessage( 'pagerating-header', "'''This page
                    lists the $1 ranked pages on the wiki.'''" );
$wgMessageCache->addMessage( 'pagerating-limitlinks', 'Show
                    up to $1 pages' );
$wgMessageCache->addMessage( 'pagerating-showing',
                    'Found $1 pages;
listing newest first:' );
$wgMessageCache->addMessage( 'pagerating-none', 'No entries
                    were found.' );
}
```

In the previous code section, we are basically extending the call-back functions
on MediaWiki by adding a new call function wfSpecialPageRating to the
Functions array. The $wgExtensionCredits array actually holds information
about the extension such as author name, extension name, URL, etc. The next
function wfSpecialPageRating adds a new special page for the PageRating class.
wgMessageCache->addMessage is used to add new messages to the wiki system
without entering them in the language file.

```
class PageRating extends IncludableSpecialPage
{
  var $limit = 50;
  function PageRating()
  {
    SpecialPage::SpecialPage( 'PageRating', '', true, false,
                        'default', true );
  }
  function execute( $par )
  {
    global $wgOut;
    $this->setLimit( $par );
    # Don't show the navigation if we're including the page
    if( !$this->mIncluding )
    {
      $this->setHeaders();
      $wgOut->addWikiText( wfMsg( 'pagerating-header',
                          $this->limit ));
      $wgOut->addHTML( $this->makeLimitLinks() );
    }
    $dbr =& wfGetDB( DB_SLAVE );
    $res = $dbr->query( "SELECT * from articlerating ORDER BY
                    articleID DESC LIMIT 0,{$this->limit}" );
    $count = $dbr->numRows( $res );
    if( $count > 0 )
    {
```

```
# Make tabled list
if( !$this->mIncluding )
$wgOut->addWikiText( wfMsg ( 'pagerating-showing', $count ) );
$wgOut->addHTML( "<br><br><table align=center border=0
          cellspacing=0 cellpadding=0 width=70%
          style='background:transparent'>\n" );
$wgOut->addHTML( "<tr><Td width=5%><B>#</td>
        <Td width=50%><B>Page Title</td><td><B> Current
        Rating</td><td><B>Number of Rating</td></tr>");
$i=1;
while( $row = $dbr->fetchObject( $res ) )
$wgOut->addHTML( $this->makeListItem ( $row, $i++ ) );
$wgOut->addHTML( "</table>\n" );
}
else
{
   $wgOut->addWikiText( wfMsg( 'pagerating-none' ) );
}
$dbr->freeResult( $res );
}
```

In this code section, we are adding a new class named PageRating, which extends the IncludableSpecialPage class. Inside the class, we declare the default limit to be 50. We then declare the default constructor for the class. In the constructor, the first parameter defines the special class name (which is PageRating for our class). The second parameter defines any restriction for the access to this class. The third one defines whether the class will be listed on the special page list. The fourth one defines the function that will be called. If it is set to false, then the execute function is automatically called, or else the function whose name is given in this parameter will be called. The next one defines the file that is to be included, and the last parameter indicates if the class is includable or not. In the execute function, we are taking one parameter, the limit of the list.

If the page is called from another page where it works as an include page, then the header will not be shown as you can see from the comments in the code. After that we query the articlerating table to fetch each article's ratings, its name, and the total number of ratings to be shown on the screen. For this, we have generated a table and shown each article on a separate row. The makeListItem function is responsible for showing the row contents and we will see it now:

```
function setLimit( $par )
{
  if( $par )
  {
      $this->limit = intval( $par );
```

```
    }
    else
    {
      global $wgRequest;
      if( $limit = $wgRequest->getIntOrNull( 'limit' ) )
      {
        $this->limit = $limit;
      }
      else
      {
        $this->limit = 50;
      }
    }
  }
  function makeListItem( $row , $i )
  {
    global $wgUser;
    $title = $row->articleName;
    $ratingpoint = $row->totalPoints;
    $totalrating = $row->totalRatings;
    $currentRating = sprintf("%.2f",$ratingpoint/$totalrating);
    if( !is_null( $title ) )
    {
      return( "<tr><td>$i.</td><td>$title</td><td align=center>
        $currentRating</td><td align=center>$totalrating</td></tr>\n");
    }
    else
    {
      return( "<!-- Invalid title "
              . htmlspecialchars( $row->page_title ) . " in namespace "
              . htmlspecialchars( $row->page_namespace ) . " -->\n" );
    }
  }
}
```

The set Limit function sets the article list limit that is set by the users. It overwrites the current limit value with the user-selected value. The makeListItem function takes the row object and listing number as parameter, and calculates the average rating for the article and returns the row string to the execute function. The last part of the special code, which creates the limit links shown on the header of the special page, is as follows:

```
function makeLimitLinks()
{
  global $wgUser;
```

```
$skin = $wgUser->getSkin();
$title = Title::makeTitle( NS_SPECIAL, 'PageRating' );
$limits = array( 10, 20, 30, 50, 100, 150 );
foreach( $limits as $limit )
{
  if( $limit != $this->limit )
  {
    $links[] = $skin->makeKnownLinkObj( $title, $limit,
                                        'limit=' . $limit );
  }
  Else
  {
    $links[] = (string)$limit;
  }
}
return( wfMsgHtml( 'pagerating-limitlinks',
                   implode( ' | ', $links ) ) );
}
}
}
else
{
  echo( "This is an extension to the MediaWiki package and cannot
                                        be run standalone.\n" );
  die( -1 );
}
?>
```

So after combining the code blocks, we have to make sure that we have saved it inside the `extensions` folder. After saving this file, we need to do one more thing. We have to add this file path at the end of the `LocalSettings.php` file in order to let the system know about our file. Here is the entry to be added:

```
include "extensions/SpecialPageRating.php";
```

Without adding this entry, our special page will not work. So this step is mandatory for *all* special page additions. After doing all this hard work, we have to click the **special pages** link from the toolbox section. We will see our special page listed on the list. The name of the page is **Article Ratings**. If we want, we can change the title to one that we desire.

If we click **Article Ratings**, then we will be taken to the following page, where all the ratings are shown. In order to write new special pages, you can always use an approach similar to the one we just took.

Custom Namespaces

We can have our own namespace, which is known as having a custom namespace. Each project or wiki can have a lot of custom namespaces as per the site's requirement. Custom namespaces are added by the administrator in need of new namespaces other than the ones defined by MediaWiki. For our site, we can have different namespaces such as story, article, novel, real-life experience, etc. In general, custom namespaces are numbered from 100.

In order to add a new custom namespace, we have to perform the following steps:

1. Pick a name for the namespace and its corresponding talk page.
   Do not include a space in the name. If required, you can use the underscore
   (_) character.

2. Pick namespace numbers appropriately. Numbers should start from after
   100. Also we should apply the following rule for talk pages: *Even numbers are
   for namespaces containing articles, odd numbers are reserved for talk pages for the
   corresponding namespace.*

3. In the `include` directory, open the `defaultsettings.php` file and copy the
   following variables into `LocalSettings.php`;

   ○ `$wgExtraNamespaces`

   ○ `$wgNamespacesWithSubpages`

   ○ `$wgNamespacesToBeSearchedDefault`

4. To `$wgExtraNamespaces`, add the name of your namespace and its talk
   page, using the names and numbers chosen in the first and second steps.
   If we want to add a new namespace named `Story` and its associated talk
   page `Story_talk`, then we have to add the following entry in the
   `Localsettings.php` file:

   ```
   $wgExtraNamespaces = array(100 => "Story", 101 => "Story_Talk");
   ```

5. If you want sub-pages, add them to `$wgNamespacesWithSubpages`, as shown
   in the following entry:

   ```
   $wgNamespacesWithSubpages = array(
                               NS_TALK            => true,
                               NS_USER            => true,
                               NS_USER_TALK       => true,
                               NS_PROJECT_TALK    => true,
                               NS_IMAGE_TALK      => true,
                               NS_MEDIAWIKI_TALK  => true,
                               NS_TEMPLATE_TALK   => true,
                               NS_HELP_TALK       => true,
                               NS_CATEGORY_TALK   => true,
                               STORY              => true,
                               STORY_TALK         => true
                           );
   ```

6. If you want to add the namespace to the search option, then you have to enter the namespace in the `$wgNamespacesToBeSearchedDefault` variable. By default, only the `main` namespace is searchable. You need to change that for your new namespace as follows:

```
$wgNamespacesToBeSearchedDefault = array(
                                    NS_MAIN      => true,
                                    STORY        => true
                                    );
```

After making the changes, save the `Localsettings.php` file. You do not have to restart the server. The change will be effected as soon as you save the file.

Change the Name of the Wiki

Sometimes you might need to change your wiki's name. It is possible to change the wiki's name at any point of time. In order to change the basic site name, we have to change the `$wgSitename` variable in the `LocalSettings.php` file to the new site name. First comment out the current name, and then add a new name as follows:

```
#$wgSitename = 'Haunted';
$wgSitename = 'Haunted - Asia';
```

Summary

This chapter was quite informative. We have learned about important file names and their functionality, hooks, and extending markup to extend the software. We have also seen how to add our own pages to the system and create some cool features. We have added new namespaces to our site.

It is always nice to see things working fine. It is, however, better to not change the core files provided by MediaWiki, because if the core files are broken, then the system will break as well, and it is always better to be on the safe side. In the next chapter we will explore maintenance of our server as well as MediaWiki.

10
MediaWiki Maintenance

One of the most important aspects of software is maintenance, and websites are no exception. Actually, for any kind of website, the maintenance requirement is very high. For a large website, the need to upgrade to newer releases and install patches is even higher. Since MediaWiki is open-source software, new versions of the software are released with bug fixes and new features on a continuous basis. In order to remain up to date, we have to synchronize our current installation with the latest one. We will focus on maintenance and other related issues in this chapter.

Deploying MediaWiki

Suppose you are maintaining a wiki server locally in an intranet facility and you now want to move it to a hosted server or to a production server. This task is known as moving the wiki server. One thing we have to remember is that we are moving the *whole* system, and are not *upgrading*. You should not confuse these two words. It is always preferable to set up the wiki locally and then move it to the main server, because your changes need to be properly tested and stabilized. To do this on a hosted server is not always feasible, as you have to change the file, upload it to the server, and then test it.

> It is always recommended to test changes locally and later move them to the main server.

In order to execute your move, you have to go through a step-wise checklist of actions to be performed:

1. Remove all test records (if any) from the database.
2. Back up the database.
3. Back up MediaWiki files.
4. Re-create the database, users, and permissions on the new server.
5. Import the database backup.
6. Import the MediaWiki files.
7. Change the configuration file.
8. Test the new site.

Let's discuss each of the steps in detail, to get a good idea about what is to be done, and when.

Remove all Test Records from the Database

If your server has been tested locally, then it is certain that it contains test data. It is always better to delete those test records before backing up the database. When you remove the records, it is better to use third-party software like phpMyAdmin, if you want to avoid writing commands in the command prompt. Also, it is a fact that hosted servers support these types of third-party tools; so getting used to this type of software is helpful.

Back Up the Database

After you have removed the test records from the database, take a full backup of the database, which includes dumping all data and the schema. If you are using phpMyAdmin, then you can create the dump very easily. You have to choose the database and click the **Export** tab in order to perform the export operation. The export will generate a `.sql` script, which we have to use on the new server.

In this book, we are not going into any details for such operations. It is recommended that you read corresponding manuals before performing anything. You can use the following URLs as reference:

http://dev.mysql.com/doc/refman/5.0/en/backup.html

http://www.php-mysql-tutorial.com/perform-mysql-backup-php.php

http://fragments.turtlemeat.com/mysql-database-backup-restore-phpmyadmin.php

Back Up MediaWiki Files

MediaWiki files exist in the directory where you have installed MediaWiki. All the extensions, images, and scripts files are inside the installed directory. Always back up the whole directory in an archive file—a ZIP or a TAR file—in order to ease the transfer between different servers.

Re-Create Database, User, and Permissions on the New Server

Since you are moving the files and database to the new server, the first task before the files are imported is to create the database and a user with appropriate permissions to access the database. User privileges on the database should include SELECT, INSERT, UPDATE, and DELETE operations.

It doesn't matter if the database doesn't have the same name as the localhost test database; it is certain that in a commercial hosting environment, where database names are usually prefixed with a hosting account username, a different database name is guaranteed. In addition, the username can differ, as can that user's password.

Import Database Backup

After creating the new database and user, we need to re-create the database and populate it with data on the destination server, which is known as **importing**. In order to perform this task, you can use a third-party tool such as phpMyAdmin or use the MySQL command line if you have command-line access to the server. Whatever the method you choose, first go through the required documentation to perform the task smoothly. After importing, the database will be populated with the required tables of MediaWiki. This will indicate that you have successfully imported the database.

Import MediaWiki Files

The most important and time-consuming part of changing servers is to move the directory files. All the files in the old server directory must be copied properly to the new host. You can use any FTP application, or the hosting service provider's web FTP to upload the files. One thing you must ensure is that you have uploaded every single file from your previous directory, because any missing file may create unwanted errors. During upload, a few files might get corrupted; you may then have to change those files as well.

Change the Configuration File

The final task of moving your wiki site is to change the configuration file in the new directory to which the site has been moved. You will need to change the `LocalSettings.php` file in order to change the database and server variables for the new host. As you already know, on a hosting server, usually we assign new database users and passwords; the configuration file should reflect such changes, otherwise our new server will not work. Here are the variables that need to be configured:

- `$IP`: Needs to be correct for the paths on the new server
- `$wgScriptPath`: Needs to be correct for the path on the new server
- `$wgDBserver`: Check the database server name is correct
- `$wgDBname`: This might have changed in a shared hosting environment
- `$wgDBuser`: This might have changed in a shared hosting environment
- `$wgDBpassword`: Check this is correct for the new user

Other than these settings, you might need to change a few other optional settings for image manipulation, math formulae, etc.

Alternatively, you can delete the `LocalSettings.php` file from your production server and reinstall MediaWiki on the production server with the information relevant to the server. You can choose to not re-create the database, and keep the existing imported database intact. When the installation is completed, the new `LocalSettings.php` file is created based on the server environment and variables. This tactic is very helpful when you move your wiki from a server where PHP runs as an Apache module to a server where PHP runs as a CGI module, and vice versa.

Test New Site

After performing all of the steps we just discussed, open the site in your browser to check if things are working properly or not. If you see any PHP or MediaWiki-related errors, such as the database connection could not be found, or a file is missing, or even a PHP setup issue, then you have to fix those according to the error types. Try to create new articles, edit articles, and upload files in order to test the new site. If you do not find any problem, then your site is ready to go live.

As your Site Grows

It is certain that your site will grow with time, and this will make you think about your server. If your audience is limited to say 100–200 users, and the average article posting is not significant, say less than 10 articles per day, then a hosted server is good for you. However, if you have thousands of visitors each day and hundreds of articles published every day, then you'll have to think along the lines of getting a dedicated server.

In MediaWiki every requested page is generated from the database, which means that every page request will generate at least one database query. You can calculate the load of the database for a well-populated server. So as visitors come and create new content, they use not just your database server space, but also your server bandwidth. As a result, the server performance will be affected, since most of the resources will be taken by the database server. In some cases, your visitors will see site not responding to their request.

To avoid such problems, you can always take some proactive steps. You can use a cache server in order to reduce the load on the database server. When a page is requested by a visitor, it is generated from the database, and a copy is stored in the cache server as well. If someone requests the same page, then the user will be served the copied version of the page from the cache server, thus avoiding a database server operation. This significantly reduces load on the database server. MediaWiki supports different types of cache technologies, such as memcache, file caching, and Squid. For this particular discussion, our focus will be on **Squid** caching.

Squid Caching

Squid is a high-performance proxy server that can also be used as an HTTP accelerator for a web server. Since MediaWiki websites are entirely generated dynamically, there is a substantial performance gain in running Squid as an HTTP accelerator for your web server. In fact, sites like Wikipedia use several Squid caches to enhance their performance. Because of this performance gain, MediaWiki has been designed to integrate closely with Squid. For example, MediaWiki will notify Squid when a page should be purged from the cache in order to be regenerated.

Squid installation, configuration, and management are not a part of the focus of this book. Our sole purpose is to let you know about the available options for improved performance. It is always recommended that you read the vendor-specific documentation to install and configure Squid. You can find a complete document about configuring Squid with MediaWiki at:

`http://meta.wikimedia.org/wiki/Squid_caching`

Maintaining MediaWiki

For maintenance purposes, MediaWiki has a range of scripts available. These scripts reside in the `maintenance` folder of the installed directory. There are many scripts inside the `maintenance` folder without proper documentation. In order to use those scripts you need to understand the purpose of the scripts by the name and also reading the comments section at the beginning of the script. If you want to run any script, you have to perform the following steps:

1. Create and modify `Adminsettings.php` from the sample file `Adminsettings.sample` in the web root directory.

2. Choose the maintenance script you want to run: `rebuildall.php` (to rebuild all files).

3. Figure out how to run PHP scripts from the command line. If you are running on a *nix system and you have PHP installed, it does not necessarily mean you have `php-cli` (the command-line interface) installed as well. You need the command-line version, and then you can run command-line PHP scripts. To verify that you can run them, type `php-version` on the command line. It should tell you the currently installed version.

4. Run the script using the command: `php name_of_script.php` (or `php5 name_of_script.php`), where `name_of_script.php` is the script you want to run in the `maintenance/` directory. An example run could be as follows:

   ```
   foo@bar:~/www/haunted/maintenance$ php refreshLinks.php
   ```

Upgrading MediaWiki

As I said before, MediaWiki is open-source software, and is popular. As a result, releases come out quite often. Sometimes releases contain bugfixes and new features, and sometimes new architecture for improved performance. Whatever the reason, we have to be up to date with the latest release for bugs, new features, and security upgrades. One bad thing about upgrading is that whatever you have changed in the MediaWiki code for your current installation, you have to make those same changes in the update as well. This is something really painful if you have made a significant number of changes in the current code base. Before upgrading, read the file release notes in order to get a picture of what has been changed in the new version. If you think that those changes are minor, then you can decide to not upgrade your current version. An upgrade to the latest release is, however, always recommended.

Summary

As we are approaching the end of the book, we are gaining more advanced and required knowledge about maintaining our software. We have learned caching, upgrading, and backup techniques for MediaWiki. This knowledge will be very helpful if you are running any wiki site as an administrator. It is always recommended to keep your site up to date with the changes and features that MediaWiki releases on a regular basis. In the course of time, MediaWiki will be enriched with new features and exclusive features for a better user experience. Here's to more people using MediaWiki and joining the collaborative world of knowledge sharing!

11
Cool Hacks

In Chapter 9, we created hacks for extending our wiki installation and have added new features to our wiki site. There are many hacks available for MediaWiki on the Internet and each hack adds a desired feature to it. In this chapter we will talk about hacks for MediaWiki and will focus on the most useful and desired extensions. We will discuss:

- Calender
- Who is Online
- YouTube
- Multi-upload
- Category Cloud
- Google Maps
- Amazon Ads

These are a few of my favorite hacks since they are very useful and easy to use. So let's begin our discussion. One thing I must mention before starting is that all these hacks are available on the MediaWiki site, under the extension category.

Calendar

With a calendar, it's easy to keep track of all important events in one place. In MediaWiki, we have one such extension, which shows the calendar for a particular month, and links for every date. You can use this hack to add events to your calendar schedule. You can have daily, weekly, monthly, quarterly, and even yearly views. The latest version of this extension can be downloaded from http://krass.com/software/.

Here are the required steps to add this extension in your site:

1. Download the ZIP file from the provided URL and unzip the file. Copy all the files into the `extensions` directory of your wiki installation.

2. Include the following line at the end of your `LocalSettings.php` file:

   ```
   include("extensions/Calendar.php");
   ```

3. In the edit page, add the following text to show the calendar on the page:

   ```
   <calendar>
   name=Calendar
   view=month
   </calendar>
   ```

It will show the calendar for current month as follows:

February						
M	T	W	T	F	S	S
			1	2	3	4
5	6	7	8	9	10	11
12	13	14	15	**16**	17	18
19	20	21	22	23	24	25
26	27	28				

Who is Online

This hack displays the number of active users (both **Guests** and **Registered** users) online at any particular time. If the time period is set to 3600 seconds (1 hour), it will show the number of unique users that have accessed the site within the last one hour.

You can download the extension from `http://www.chekmate.org/wiki/index.php/MW:_Whos_Online_Extension`.

Here are the required steps to add this extension in your site:

1. Add one new table in your database, named `online`. If your database uses a prefix, then add the prefix before the table name. Here is the SQL code for creating the table:

```
CREATE TABLE `online`
                (
                    `userid` int(5) NOT NULL default '0',
```

```
`username` varchar(255) NOT NULL default '',
`timestamp` varchar(255) NOT NULL default ''
)
TYPE=MyISAM;
```

 If you do not want to create the table by yourself then this script can also do that for you.

But you have to make sure that the database user must have the the previlege to create tables.

2. Copy the code from the provided URL and save the file as `WhosOnline.php` inside the extensions folder.

3. Add the following to the end of `LocalSettings.php`:

    ```
    require_once("extensions/WhosOnline.php");
    ```

4. Add the following code in your wiki page:

    ```
    <b>Users Online</b>: <whosonline></whosonline>
    ```

And this will produce the following output:

> **Users Online**: Guests: 1 Registered: 1 (**GhostWriter**)

YouTube

YouTube is the most popular video-sharing website on the Internet. You can use this site to upload and share your videos with others. Wouldn't it be great to include a YouTube video inside your wiki page! MediaWiki has an extension to integrate these videos on your wiki page, which can be downloaded from the following page:

```
http://www.mediawiki.org/wiki/Extension:YouTube_(Iubito)
```

Here are the required steps to add this extension in your site:

1. Download the file and put it inside the `extensions` folder of your wiki installation.

2. Include the following line at the end of your `LocalSettings.php` file:

    ```
    include('extensions/youTube.php');
    ```

3. In the edit page, add the following text to show a horse video on the page:

    ```
    <youtube>6n8IUNUEp3g</youtube>
    ```

This will take you to the following page:

Multi-Upload

On many occasions, you might have felt the need to upload more than one file at a time in the wiki, especially while uploading a photo album. But MediaWiki does not allow us to upload more than one file at a time. We can solve this problem using the Multi-Upload extension. This extension can be downloaded from the following URL:

```
http://www.wikihow.com/x/multipleupload.tar
```

Here are the steps that you have to perform to make it work:

1. Download the file and put it inside the `extensions` folder of your wiki installation.

2. Include the following line at the end of your `LocalSettings.php` file:
   ```
   require_once('extensions/SpecialMultipleUpload.php');
   ```

3. Now we have to put the special upload link on any page or toolbox section we want. If we want to add it in any of our page then we have to write the following code on that page:
   ```
   [[Special:MultipleUpload.]]
   ```

This will link to the special upload page shown in the following screenshot:

Upload Files

Upload multiple files here.

Choose 'Browse' and select each file you wish to upload. You can upload from 1 to 5 files at a time.

You can enter an optional **Destination filename** and provide a **Summary** describing your photo.

Inappropriate images will be deleted immediately, see the Image Deletion Policy

Source filename:	**Destination filename:**	**Summary:**
[_____] [Browse...]	[_____]	[_____]
[_____] [Browse...]	[_____]	[_____]
[_____] [Browse...]	[_____]	[_____]
[_____] [Browse...]	[_____]	[_____]
[_____] [Browse...]	[_____]	[_____]

☐ **Watch this page** ☐ **Ignore any warnings**

[**Upload file**]

By default, you can only upload 5 files at a time. But we can change this number by changing the `$wgMaxUploadFiles` variable inside the `SpecialMultipleUpload.php` file to a number of our choice.

Category Cloud

A tag cloud is a text-based representation of content tags used across a website. In MediaWiki we can use such cloud for categories, and can the set minimum and maximum size of the font of the cloud. The category cloud is based on sub-categories and not on articles. Only sub-categories under a top-level category will be shown in the cloud. Suppose you have one category named Ghost**Sections** and under the category there are sub-categories — **Exalted, Fan Fictions, Fedora, Novels, Stories**, and **Websites** — then you can create a tag cloud for the category GhostSections, which will look like the image below. You can also set the order of the category cloud based on category name or number of articles under each category.

Exalted Fan Fictions Fedora Novels Stories Websites

You can find the category cloud extension code at the following URL:

`http://mfgames.com/svn/mediawiki/category-cloud/category-cloud.php`

Here are the steps that you have to perform to make it work:

1. Download the file and put it inside the `extensions` folder of your wiki installation.

2. Include the following line at the end of your `LocalSettings.php` file:

   ```
   include("extensions/category-cloud.php");
   ```

3. Write the following code in any page where you want to show the category cloud:

   ```
   <category-cloud category="CategoryOfTopics"></category-cloud>
   ```

Google Maps

Showing a map on your site is always great way to present information. The Google map extension gives us the opportunity to use this powerful Google tool in our wiki. We can add a map of any place in our wiki. We can use the find street address option from the built-in search facility of the Google map from our wiki. For the latest code for the Google map extension we have to visit the following URL:

`http://www.mediawiki.org/wiki/Extension:Google_Maps`

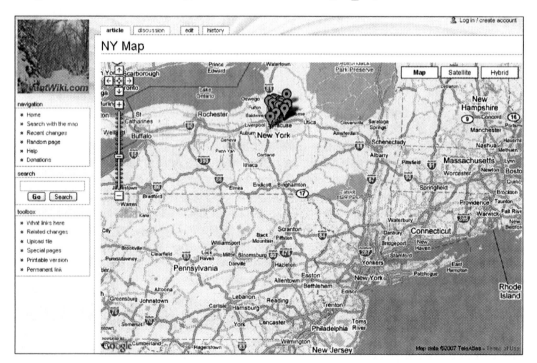

Here are the steps that you have to perform to make it work:

1. Download the file and unzip it. Put the folder inside the `extensions` folder of your wiki installation.

2. Include the following lines at the end of your `LocalSettings.php` file:

```
$wgGoogleMapsKey = "your map api key";
require_once( "extensions/GoogleMaps/GoogleMaps.php" );
```

   You have to put your Google map API key in the `$wgGoogleMapsKey` variable. You can have your own site map key from `http://maps.google.com/apis/maps/`. To get the API key type the full URL of your site and you will be provided with a key. Copy the key and paste it to the `Localsettings.php` file.

3. You have to use the `<googlemap></googlemap>` tag to show your desired map in your wiki page. You have to put the latitude and longitude inside the `<googlemap>` tag.

Amazon Ads

If you are associated with Amazon.com's affiliate marketing program then this extension would prove very useful to you. By displaying Amazon's product you can earn revenue for your site. This extension is available at:

`http://www.mediawiki.org/wiki/Extension:Amazon_Associate_Ads`

Here are the steps that you have to perform to make it work:

1. Download the file and put the folder inside the `extensions` folder of your wiki installation.

2. Include the following line at the end of your `LocalSettings.php` file:

```
include( "extensions/AmazonExt.php" );
```

3. You have to use the following code to show the ads in the wiki page you intend to show them:

```
<amazon>
        amazon_ad_tag = "your_associate_ID";
        amazon_ad_width = "728";
        amazon_ad_height="90";
        amazon_ad_logo="hide";
        amazon_ad_link_target ="new";
        amazon_ad_border="hide";
        amazon_ad_include="computer; ghost+book;"
</amazon>
```

You have to enter your Amazon associate ID as `amazon_ad_tag`. You will receive the associate ID once you sign up for the Amazon associates program.

Summary

Finally we have reached the end of this book. We have learned almost everything required to edit, customize, configure, maintain, and modify our wiki site. One thing you must remember while working with any open-source project is that there is nothing called the 'end'. With time new features and extensions keep coming. So it is always better to keep yourself updated with the latest modifications in any technology that you are using. Hacks, like the ones in this chapter and many more, can be found on the MediaWiki site. So, keep yourself updated with the MediaWiki site and make your contributions to online communities.

Index

[PACKT]
PUBLISHING

Thank you for buying
MediaWiki Administrators'
Tutorial Guide

Packt Open Source Project Royalties

When we sell a book written on an Open Source project, we pay a royalty directly to that project. Therefore by purchasing MediaWiki Administrators' Tutorial Guide, Packt will have given some of the money received to the MediaWiki project.

In the long term, we see ourselves and you—customers and readers of our books—as part of the Open Source ecosystem, providing sustainable revenue for the projects we publish on. Our aim at Packt is to establish publishing royalties as an essential part of the service and support a business model that sustains Open Source.

If you're working with an Open Source project that you would like us to publish on, and subsequently pay royalties to, please get in touch with us.

Writing for Packt

We welcome all inquiries from people who are interested in authoring. Book proposals should be sent to authors@packtpub.com. If your book idea is still at an early stage and you would like to discuss it first before writing a formal book proposal, contact us; one of our commissioning editors will get in touch with you.

We're not just looking for published authors; if you have strong technical skills but no writing experience, our experienced editors can help you develop a writing career, or simply get some additional reward for your expertise.

About Packt Publishing

Packt, pronounced 'packed', published its first book "Mastering phpMyAdmin for Effective MySQL Management" in April 2004 and subsequently continued to specialize in publishing highly focused books on specific technologies and solutions.

Our books and publications share the experiences of your fellow IT professionals in adapting and customizing today's systems, applications, and frameworks. Our solution-based books give you the knowledge and power to customize the software and technologies you're using to get the job done. Packt books are more specific and less general than the IT books you have seen in the past. Our unique business model allows us to bring you more focused information, giving you more of what you need to know, and less of what you don't.

Packt is a modern, yet unique publishing company, which focuses on producing quality, cutting-edge books for communities of developers, administrators, and newbies alike. For more information, please visit our website: www.PacktPub.com.

Printed in the United States
86590LV00005B/49/A